THE RISE
OF TRUMP

THE RISE
OF TRUMP

AMERICA'S **AUTHORITARIAN** SPRING

Matthew C. MacWilliams

AUSTIN D. SARAT *Series Editor*

Conceived as a "digital pamphlet" series, titles in *Public Works* seek out and make available to a wide audience of readers the perspectives of leading scholars in the humanities on questions rising to significance in our public conversation, and demanding more discerning examination and penetrating insight. Shorter than monographs, these works will offer both authors and readers the freedom of long-form essays and the tools of digital media to see through the lens of the human experience the seemingly intractable questions confronting a complex, deeply interconnected, and sometimes shockingly violent world.

Essays published in *Public Works* series are available as open-access works of scholarship, immediately and freely available to readers and thinkers everywhere. As digital works, they will be published to the web and also downloadable to a variety of reading devices.

THE RISE OF TRUMP
America's Authoritarian Spring

Published by The Amherst College Press
Robert Frost Library • Amherst, Massachusetts

ISBN 978-1-943208-02-9 paperback
ISBN 978-1-943208-03-6 electronic book

Library of Congress Control Number: 2016954388

Table of Contents

Acknowledgments

This book benefited substantially from the comments of two anonymous reviewers, to whom I here record my deep gratitude. Thanks are also due to the Department of Political Science at the University of Massachusetts; and to Dr. Brian Schaffner and Dr. Tatishe Nteta for their assistance with survey construction and analysis.

"... the dynamics of American development cannot simply be seen as a rising tide of liberalizing forces progressively submerging contrary beliefs and practices... the currents pulling toward fuller expression of alleged natural and cultural inequalities have also always won victories."

Rogers M. Smith
"Beyond Tocqueville, Myrdal, and Hartz:
The Multiple Traditions in America"

Introduction

On June 16, 2015, Donald Trump descended the gilded Trump Tower escalator, strode to the podium, and announced his candidacy for president of the United States. His rambling speech stretched for nearly an hour. It was described as outrageous, incoherent, and xenophobic.[1] Trump warned "our enemies are getting stronger and stronger... and we as a country are getting weaker." He accused Mexico of purposely "sending people that have lots of problems" across our borders. And then he uttered the first words that set him far apart for all other major candidates running for office at the time: These people "are bringing drugs. They're bringing crime. They're rapists."[2]

Trump's allegation that Latino immigrants are drug dealers and rapists was not a slip of the tongue. It is an integral part of his worldview and message. In Trump's us-versus-them narrative, "the other" is attacking us from without and weakening us from within as our leaders stand by clueless and ineffectual. He asks, "[h]ow stupid are our leaders... How stupid are these politicians to allow this to happen?" To Trump, the politicians are not only weak and incompetent; they are also "morally corrupt." They are selling us "down the drain," and they are "controlled fully by the lobbyists, by the donors, and by the special interests, fully."

---

1. Sally Kohn, "Trump's Outrageous Mexico Remarks," CNN.com, June 18, 2015, http://www.cnn.com/2015/06/17/opinions/kohn-donald-trump-announcement/; Reid Epstein and Heather Haddon, "Donald Trump Vows to Disrupt Crowded GOP Presidential Race," *Wall Street Journal*, June 16, 2015, http://www.wsj.com/articles/donald-trump-to-unveil-plans-for-2016-presidential-race-1434448982; Kathleen Hennessey, "Donald Trump enters race, and GOP wonders: Presidency or reality TV?," *Los Angeles Times*, June 16, 2015, http://www.latimes.com/nation/la-na-gop-trump-20150615-story.html.

2. *Time*, "Here's Donald Trump's Presidential Announcement Speech," June 16, 2015, http://time.com/3923128/donald-trump-announcement-speech/. Trump ended this statement saying, "And some, I assume, are good people."

Beset by external enemies, threatened by fifth column foes, and abandoned by an incompetent government and corrupt politicians, Trump proclaims that our country doesn't win anymore, saying "[s]adly, the American dream is dead." The only leader who can revive it is, of course, Trump. "But if I get elected president I will bring it back bigger and better and stronger than ever before, and we will make America great again."

Politico, a leading news organization dedicated to covering politics in the United States and around the world, called Trump's announcement "one of the more bizarre spectacles of the 2016 political season thus far," and, foreshadowing the media circus that was to follow, "one of the most entertaining."[3] Political elites wrote off Trump's presidential bid as a fool's errand pursued by a narcissist. And the national media settled in to cover what was anticipated to be a short-lived, ultimately unsuccessful, but rating- and revenue-generating rerun of *Celebrity Apprentice*.

The day Donald Trump announced his campaign for president, three Republican Party insider favorites—former Governor Jeb Bush, Governor Scott Walker, and Senator Marco Rubio—led the Republican presidential field.[4] What political scientists call the "invisible primary" appeared in full tilt with party insiders well in control of the nomination process.[5] One month and two days later, Trump led Bush, Walker's support was stagnant, and Rubio had faded.[6] To the dismay, then alarm, and finally the horror of the Republican Party establish-

---

3. Adam Lerner, "The 10 best lines from Donald Trump's announcement speech," June 16, 2015, Politico, http://www.politico.com/story/2015/06/donald-trump-2016-announcement-10-best-lines-119066.

4. RealClearPolitics, "2016 Republican Presidential Nomination," http://www.realclearpolitics.com/epolls/2016/president/us/2016_republican_presidential_nomination-3823.html. The RealClearPolitics (RCP) poll-of-polls average on June 16, 2016, shows Bush, Walker and Rubio in a virtual tie with each garnering between 10 and 10.8 percent of the vote.

5. Marty Cohen, David Karol, Hans Noel, and John Zaller, *The Party Decides: Presidential Nominations Before and After Reform* (Chicago: University of Chicago Press, 2008).

6. RealClearPolitics, "2016 Republican Presidential Nomination." On July 16, 2016, Bush led the RCP poll-of-polls average with 15.5 percent followed by Trump at 15 percent. Walker's support was at 9 percent, and Rubio's support had fallen to just 6 percent. On July 18, 2016, Trump surpassed Bush.

ment,[7] Trump led the RealClearPolitics Republican primary poll-of-polls average every day from July 18, 2015 onward.[8]

While Trump's ascendancy says something particular about his celebrity and showmanship, it says much more about the resonance of his rhetoric. Trump's message struck what Tony Schwartz once called a "responsive chord" in America.[9] Those who responded, and are still responding today, do not fit neatly into the simplistic, comforting, and condescending elite meme that Trump supporters are the "usual suspects"—working class, white, dispossessed males.[10] Activated by Trump's message and bluster, driven by threats real and imagined, and catalyzed by the media's incessant repetition of both,[11] a group responsive to a particular style of discourse—American authoritarians—rallied to Trump's banner, providing him with a resilient base of support relatively impervious to attack and large enough, after years of partisan shifts in the electorate, to dominate a multi-candidate Republican primary contest.[12]

7. On January 21, 2016, the *National Review*, perhaps the American conservative movement's most influential publication, published commentaries from twenty leading conservatives each arguing that Trump must not become the Republican nominee for president. *National Review's* lead editorial in that issue warned that "Trump is a philosophically unmoored political opportunist who would trash the broad conservative ideological consensus within the GOP in favor of a free-floating populism with strongman overtones." "Against Trump," *National Review*, January 21, 2016, http://www.nationalreview.com/article/430137/donald-trump-conservative-movement-menace. Newt Gingrich, the former Republican Speaker of the House of Representative, agreed with the National Review's assessment saying that Donald Trump "is not a conservative." Jim Geraghty, "Newt: 'National Review's right. Trump's not a conservative," *National Review*, July 14, 2016, http://www.nationalreview.com/corner/437836/newt-national-reviews-right-trumps-not-conservative.

8. http://www.realclearpolitics.com/epolls/2016/president/us/2016_republican_presidential_nomination-3823.html

9. Tony Schwartz, *The Responsive Chord* (Garden City, N.Y.: Anchor Press/Doubleday, 1973).

10. See William Galston, "Trump Rides a Blue-Collar Wave," *Wall Street Journal*, November 17, 2015, http://www.wsj.com/articles/trump-rides-a-blue-collar-wave-1447803248 and Nate Silver, "The Mythology of Trump's 'Working Class' Support," FiveThirtyEight, May 3, 2016, http://fivethirtyeight.com/features/the-mythology-of-trumps-working-class-support/.

11. Nicholas Confessore and Karen Yourish, "2 Billion Worth of Free Media for Donald Trump," *New York Times*, March 15, 2016, http://www.nytimes.com/2016/03/16/upshot/measuring-donald-trumps-mammoth-advantage-in-free-media.html.

12. Individuals with a disposition to authoritarianism demonstrate a fear of "the other" as well as a readiness to follow and obey strong leaders. They tend to see the world in black-and-white terms. They are by definition attitudinally inflexible and rigid. And once

Beginning with his June announcement speech, Trump's candidacy was an unapologetic clarion call to Americans disposed to authoritarianism. The shooting of Kathryn Steinle in San Francisco by an illegal immigrant on July 1, 2015 amplified Trump's warnings of the risk posed by "the others" in our society. It also provided Trump with a cudgel against Jeb Bush's "they come out of love" immigration policy and, to some Americans, further proof of the government's incompetence and inability to secure the borders and protect the country. Later that year, on November 13, terrorist attacks in Paris created an inflection point reinforcing Trump's *casus belli* against Muslims and increased the momentum of his campaign. And the December 2, 2015 San Bernardino terrorist shootings appeared to provide proof positive that Trump's warnings were fact, not fiction.

Amplified by 24/7 news coverage, the pervasive messaging of social media platforms like Twitter and Facebook, and mass rally displays of power and unity, Trump's siren call reached—and was answered by—American authoritarians. To them, Trump's warnings are prophetic and manifest. "The other" is among us. "The other" is a danger. Political correctness is more than a misguided moral narrative; it is weakening our grasp of basic common sense, and increasingly undermines our safety and our prosperity. In a field of candidates beholden to establishment values only Trump is telling it like it is, and uniquely offers the skill and will to do what is necessary to protect Americans and make America great again.

Trump triumphed over sixteen rivals for the Republican nomination by espousing ascriptive, punitive policies on immigration and deportation, adopting a strongman tone and swagger, insulting "the others" in society, disregarding facts, and replacing consistency with unpredictability. He flaunted norms of civil political discourse by taunting opponents and the media, darkly warning of violence, cyberbullying critics, issuing thinly-veiled threats, and inciting supporters at his mass rallies to violence. As a candidate, his deportment was

---

they have identified friend from foe, they hold tight to their conclusions. This intransigent behavioral tendency of authoritarians may help explain why Trump's support can seem, as a strategist for Marco Rubio complained in the *New York Times*, like "granite." Jeremy Peters, "Marco Rubio's Camp Sees Opening if Donald Trump Wins in Iowa," *New York Times*, January 28, 2016, http://www.nytimes.com/2016/01/29/us/politics/marco-rubios-camp-sees-opening-if-donald-trump-wins-in-iowa.html.

unthinkable from the day he announced. Then, its shock value became entertainment as his message struck home with those Americans predisposed to authoritarianism, catalyzing a loyal base of support that was both unassailable and decisive.

But is Trump's success in the Republican nominating process demonstrably different from what has occurred in America's past? Does it represent simply part of the tug of war between illiberal and democratic American traditions that will be bested in the general election and relegated to the fringe? Or is Trump's remarkable run, which surprised almost every pundit, commentator, and political insider in America and the world, something quite different? Is it a bellwether of change, a harbinger of a renewed competition between democracy and totalitarianism that mirrors the changes occurring across the world in China, Hungary, Russia, Turkey, France, Slovakia, Hungary, and the Middle East? Is it the outcome of which historian Rogers Smith warned when he wrote, "the novelties and scientific doctrines of the Gilded Age and the Progressive Era should alert us to the possibility that new intellectual systems and political forces defending racial and gender inequalities may yet gain increased power in our time"?[13]

Trump's success in the Republican primaries this year is demonstrably different from what has occurred in America's political past, at least since Andrew Jackson was elected president. It is the rise of American authoritarianism—America's Authoritarian Spring. And it is the product of the confluence of a number of long-term political and demographic trends together with unique factors that created the conditions for a Trump-like candidacy to flourish. In what follows, I dissect the different factors that provided fertile soil for Trumpism to take root. But I leave it up to you to determine if Trump's rise is a time-bound anomaly or a foreshadowing of the future of American politics.

I begin by defining what I mean by the term "ascriptive" and tracing, quite briefly, some of the linkages between America's ascriptive past and Trump's present campaign. Next, I turn to defining authoritarianism and discuss how it has been studied, how it is measured, and the important role threat plays in its activation. I will then present

---

13. Rogers M. Smith, "Beyond Tocqueville, Myrdal, and Hartz: The Multiple Traditions in America," *American Political Science Review* 87(3) (September 1993), 563.

the statistical evidence that Trump's core supporters in the days leading up to the Iowa and New Hampshire contests were dispositionally and behaviorally authoritarian. With this background in view, I will turn to an examination of the unique conditions that made the 2016 primaries conducive to Trump's candidacy. There have always been Americans predisposed to authoritarians in the electorate; what made the 2016 primaries different? I will conclude with a brief summary and what I think is a pertinent question about the future: Which road will America choose in November? Will we choose an ascriptive path, the path of republicanism, or the path of liberalism? All three paths are a part of our tradition. Which will prevail? The answer may be as important to the United States—and to the world—as any election in our recent history.

America's Ascriptive Tradition and Donald Trump

Trump's unvarnished us-versus-them rhetoric is not new to America. As Rogers Smith reminds us, the liberal and republican traditions celebrated by Tocqueville, Myrdal, and Hartz are just one part of the story of American political development. There is another tradition— an ascriptive tradition—that ascribes to specific groups, whether defined in terms of race, ethnicity, creed, gender, sexual orientation, or some other distinguishing characteristic—qualities that are seen to justify unequal treatment.[14] This tradition has existed throughout America's history, contending "that the nation's political and economic structures should formally reflect natural and cultural inequalities, even at the cost of violating doctrines of universal rights."[15] Racism, sexism, and nativism are expressions of this tradition. So are some of the darkest moments in American history—events that have raised

---

14. Smith, "Beyond Tocqueville, Myrdal, and Hartz," 563 (esp. footnote 4). Smith defines the ascriptive tradition as follows: "Adherents of what I term ascriptive Americanist traditions believe true Americans are in some way 'chosen' by God, history, or nature to possess superior moral and intellectual traits, often associated with race and gender. Hence many Americanists believe that nonwhites and women should be governed as subjects of second-class citizens, denied full market rights, and sometimes excluded from the nation altogether."

15. Smith, 550.

fundamental questions about the nation's core values, and are echoed disturbingly in Trump's rhetoric and proposed policies.

For example, the forced removal of members of the so-called Five Civilized Tribes from the American southeast under the Indian Removal Act of 1830, culminating in the eviction of the Cherokee nation from Georgia from 1838 through 1839 (the "Trail of Tears"), all countenanced by President Jackson and carried out by President Van Buren (despite being prohibited by the Supreme Court),[16] is the historic forbear of Trump's call to deport 11 million illegal immigrants. Similarly, the wholesale rounding up and internment of Japanese Americans in 1942, authorized by Franklin Roosevelt's Executive Order 9066, is a more recent example of the disturbing exercise of state power against "the other"—and the abrogation of "the other's" fundamental rights and liberties—justified by the perceived need for security.[17]

Trump's admonition that Islam poses a threat to America resembles warnings issued of Catholic plots to undermine American democracy from the 1830s through John F. Kennedy's campaign for president in 1960.[18] Trump's anti-immigrant rhetoric is a contemporary manifestation of the Chinese Exclusion Act of 1882, described by Smith as "the first repudiation of America's long history of open immigration."[19] And Trump's call for the establishment of a database to track American Muslims—as well as special police patrols in Muslim neighborhoods to surveil them—eerily echoes Joseph McCarthy's Red Scare witch hunt for Communists in American government and society in the 1950s.[20]

---

16. The court's decision effectively invalidating the Indian Removal Act is *Worcester v. Georgia*. For the court's approach to the case, see Stephen Breyer, *Making our Democracy Work: A Judge's View* (New York: Alfred A. Knopf, 2010).

17. As the Roman statesman Marcus Tullius Cicero is said to have commented, "inter arma enim silent lex" ("in times of war the law is silent").

18. Richard Hofstader, "The Paranoid Style in American Politics," *Harper's Magazine* 229 (November 1964), 79–81. On the anti-Catholic opposition to Kennedy's 1960 presidency, see especially A&E Networks, "JFK: Catholic for President," History, http://www.history.com/topics/us-presidents/john-f-kennedy/videos/jfk-and-the-pope.

19. Smith, "Beyond Tocqueville, Myrdal, and Hartz," 560.

20. Ironically, Roy Cohn, who served as Senator McCarthy's Chief Counsel on the Senate Permanent Subcommittee on Investigations in its investigations of the infiltration of Communists into the U.S. government and society, was hired by Trump and became his mentor. Michelle Dean, "A mentor in shamelessness: The man who taught Trump

Whether it is the original system of Jim Crow, given legal legitimacy in the "separate but equal" doctrine of *Plessy v. Ferguson*, or the system of mass incarceration of black men Michelle Alexander has dubbed the "New Jim Crow";[21] George Wallace's 1968 "segregation now, segregation tomorrow, segregation forever" campaign for president, or Trump's non-disavowal disavowal of the Ku Klux Klan[22]—all have deep roots in America's ascriptive tradition. The tradition flows through American history, and no group of Americans—racial, ethnic, political, or socioeconomic—are immune from its practice.[23] But it seems hard to dispute that the historic, all-time high-water mark of the ascriptive tradition is a presidential candidate whose politics were "characterized by intensely personal leadership, charismatic appeals to his followers, demands for extreme personal loyalty, and a violent antipathy against all who disagreed with him."[24]

That candidate is not Donald Trump. It was President Andrew Jackson.

The worldviews and rhetoric of President Jackson, Senator Huey Long, Governor George Wallace, Senator Joe McCarthy, Speechwriter Patrick Buchanan, and Donald Trump all have embraced America's ascriptive tradition. Their political approach exemplifies what historian Richard Hofstadter called "the paranoid style in American politics," an "old and recurrent phenomenon in our public life" that "has a greater

---

the power of publicity," *The Guardian*, April 20, 2016, http://www.theguardian.com/us-news/2016/apr/20/roy-cohn-donald-trump-joseph-mccarthy-rosenberg-trial

21. Michelle Alexander, *The New Jim Crow: Mass Incarceration in the Age of Colorblindness* (New York: The New Press, 2010).

22. At first, Trump did not disavow Duke and the KKK. (Eric Bradner, "Donald Trump stumbles on David Duke, KKK," CNN.com, February 29, 2016, http://www.cnn.com/2016/02/28/politics/donald-trump-white-supremacists/.) Then, after a media firestorm, he disavowed him. ("Trump denounces David Duke, KKK," CNN.com, March 3, 2016, http://www.cnn.com/2016/03/03/politics/donald-trump-disavows-david-duke-kkk/.) See also Evan Osnos, "Donald Trump and the Ku Klux Klan: A History," *The New Yorker*, February 20, 2016, http://www.newyorker.com/news/news-desk/donald-trump-and-the-ku-klux-klan-a-history.

23. As Smith writes, "Cherokees enslaved Blacks, champions of women's rights disparaged Blacks and immigrants, and Blacks have often been hostile toward Hispanics and other new immigrants. White men, in turn, have been prominent among those combating invidious exclusions as well as those imposing them." Smith, "Beyond Tocqueville, Myrdal, and Hartz," 558.

24. David Fischer, *Albion's Seed: Four British Folkways in America* (New York: Oxford University Press, 1989), 849.

affinity for bad causes than good" and "has been frequently linked with movements of suspicious discontent."[25]

But it is Hofstadter's account of the message and manners of the paranoid spokesman, written more than half a century ago, that rings so true today in Donald Trump's candidacy. As Hofstadter writes,

> The paranoid spokesman…traffics in the birth and death of whole worlds, whole political orders, whole systems of human values. He is always manning the barricades of civilization… [T]he paranoid is a militant leader. He does not see social conflict as something to be mediated and compromised, in the manner of the working politician. Since what is at stake is always a conflict between absolute good and absolute evil, what is necessary is not compromise but the will to fight things out to the finish…. [The] enemy is clearly delineated…. Very often the enemy is held to possess some especially effective source of power: he controls the press; he has unlimited funds; he has a new secret for influencing the mind….[26]

Trump's candidacy is positioned as a campaign to make America great again: to reestablish America's rightful, exceptional place in the world order, fight against the barbarism of ISIS and others who do not share our civilized values, and duel with corrupt interests within who undermine America, including the incompetent leaders who have mismanaged it.

Hofstadter's depiction of the paranoid style was not prescient; it was pattern recognition. It is (and indeed it describes itself as) the identification of an approach repeated throughout American political development. Even so, the recent success of the Trumpist manifestation of the paranoid style is demonstrably different from what has occurred in our recent history. The last major campaign steeped in ascriptive politics was Pat Buchanan's insurgent, anti-immigration, and anti-gay attack on sitting Republican President George H. W. Bush in 1992. In that effort, Buchanan won no primaries—but gained 23 percent of the overall Republican vote in the nominating process. Four years later, speaking two days before the New Hampshire primary while running for the Republican nomination in an open field, Buchanan implored Americans (who accepted Buchanan's ironic label of "peasants") to pick up their pitchforks and storm the castle pro-

---

25. Hofstader, "The Paranoid Style in American Politics," 77.

26. Ibid., 82, 85.

tecting the party's elite.[27] In this second effort Buchanan won one primary and garnered almost exactly the same number of votes—3.1 million—roughly 21 percent of the total votes cast in the GOP's 1996 nominating process.[28]

By comparison, Trump dispatched with Governor Jeb Bush, President Bush's heir apparent son and the choice of the party establishment, in less than a month. He led the Republican delegate count from the night of the New Hampshire primary election, and the national Republican poll-of-polls average for the entire year leading up to the July 2016 convention. Trump won 36 states, was the choice of over 14 million Americans (or 45 percent of Republican voters), and walked into the Republican convention in Cleveland as the first contemporary nominee of a major party to win with a message imbued with and thoroughly rooted in America's ascriptive tradition.

In the end, Trump's ascriptive message and manner activated American authoritarians to support his candidacy, providing him with a virtually unassailable base and insuperable advantage in the Republican nominating contest. However, before turning to the evidence that supports this hypothesis, let me provide a modicum of background on the study, definition, activation, and measurement of authoritarianism.

The Study of Authoritarianism

Published in 1950, *The Authoritarian Personality* marks the beginning of the scholarly exploration of authoritarianism. Its investigation into the individual, psychological roots of the Fascist nightmare that descended on Europe launched two thousand studies and hundreds

---

27. See *The Economist*, "Pitchfork politics," January 2, 2016, http://www.economist. com/news/united-states/21684799-pioneer-trump-style-populism-wonders-if-it-can-succeed-todays-america-pitchfork and Joel Achenbach, "Outsiders: Trump, Bernie, Ted Cruz and the Peasants with Pitchforks," *Washington Post*, August 13, 2015, https://www.washingtonpost.com/news/achenblog/wp/2015/08/12/campaign-2016-trump-bernie-and-the-peasants-with-pitchforks/.

28. In 1996, Buchanan won the New Hampshire primary, caucuses in Missouri and Louisiana, and the Alaska straw poll. He lost the Republican nomination to Senator Bob Dole.

of academic careers.[29] While the methodology of *The Authoritarian Personality* was quickly questioned[30] and then rejected,[31] its core observation that prejudice is a generalized attitude in those individuals who are intolerant—an "entire way of thinking about those who are 'different' "[32]—is the foundation on which the studies of ethnocentrism and authoritarianism that followed are based.

From the observation that anti-Semites were also predisposed toward intolerance to others, the authors of *The Authoritarian Personality* hypothesized that the systemic prejudice observed in some individuals could be measured by a series of questions probing nine distinct, covarying traits. Answers to these questions could be summed and arrayed across a scale—what Adorno and his colleagues called the F-scale, in which F stands for fascism.[33] The psychological dimension estimated by the F-scale was then dubbed the authoritarian personality, and became the name of what quickly assumed status as a groundbreaking book.

The scientifically unfalsifiable basis of *The Authoritarian Personality*, faulty design of F-scale questions that created answer bias through acquiescent responses, and the multidimensional reality of the F-scale's intended unidimensional output, all led to withering criticism of *The*

29. Theodor W. Adorno, Else Frenkel–Burnswik, Daniel J. Levinson, and R. Nevitte Sanford, *The Authoritarian Personality* (New York: Harper and Brothers, 1950). Forty years after the publication of *The Authoritarian Personality*, more than 2,000 papers and studies on authoritarianism had been written; see Jos D. Meloen, Gert Van der Linden, and Hans De Witte, "A Test of the Approaches of Adorno et al., Lederer and Altemeyer of Authoritarianism in Belgian Flanders: A Research Note," *Political Psychology* 17(4)(1996), 643-56.

30. See, for example, Herbert Hyman and Paul B. Sheatsley, "The Authoritarian Personality—A Methodological Critique," in Richard Christie and Marie Jahoda, eds., *Studies in the Scope and Method of "The Authoritarian Personality": Continuities in Social Research* (Glencoe, Ill.; Free Press, 1954); and Seymour Martin Lipset, Political Man: *The Social Bases of Politics* (Garden City, N.Y.: Doubleday, 1960).

31. See, for example, Jos D. Meloen, Gert Van der Linden, and Hans De Witte, "A Test of the Approaches of Adorno et al., Lederer and Altemeyer of Authoritarianism in Belgian Flanders: A Research Note"; Karen Stenner, *The Authoritarian Dynamic* (Cambridge: Cambridge University Press, 2005); Marc Hetherington and Jonathan Weiler, *Authoritarianism and Polarization in American Politics* (Cambridge: Cambridge University Press, 2009).

32. David G. Meyers, *Social Psychology*, 10th ed. (Boston: McGraw-Hill, 2010), 230.

33. It is also called the California F-scale.

Authoritarian Personality's methodology.[34] It also led to new attempts to measure authoritarianism. These new measurement approaches include the Dogmatism scale,[35] Balanced F-scales,[36] the Wilson-Patterson Conservatism scale,[37] the Right-wing authoritarian scale,[38] and the child rearing battery of questions I employ.[39]

Today, much of the extensive scholarly literature on authoritarianism concludes that it is inextricably linked to political conservatism.[40] Some social scientists consider authoritarianism the psychological basis of conservatism.[41] Others describe it as a virulent variety of political conservatism.[42]

But contemporary scholar Karen Stenner makes a critical and welcome distinction between authoritarianism and conservativism. She argues that while authoritarianism is "an aversion" to different "people and beliefs," status quo conservatism "is an aversion to… change,"

34. In addition to those listed in note 31 supra, see Richard Christie, "Authoritarianism Re-Examined," in Richard Christie and Marie Jahoda, eds., *Studies in the Scope and Method of "The Authoritarian Personality."*

35. Milton Rokeach, *The Open and Closed Mind* (New York: Basic Books, 1960).

36. John J. Ray, "A New Balanced F Scale and Its Relation to Social Class," *Australian Psychologist* 7(3) (November 1972), 155–66.

37. Glenn D. Wilson and John R. Patterson, "A New Measure of Conservatism," *British Journal of Social and Clincal Psychology* 7(4) (December 1968), 264–269, DOI 10.1111/j.2044-8260.1968.tb00568.x

38. Robert Altemeyer, *Right-Wing Authoritarianism* (Winnipeg, Man.: University of Manitoba Press, 1981).

39. Matthew C. MacWilliams, "American Authoritarianism in Black and White." Ph.D. dissertation, University of Massachusetts at Amherst, 2016.

40. In addition to the works of Adorno et al., Christie, Hetherington and Weiler, and Stenner cited above, this includes Stanley Feldman and Karen Stenner, "Perceived Threat and Authoritarianism," *Political Psychology* 18(4) (December 1997), 741–70; Donald R. Kinder and Cindy D. Kam, *Us Against Them: Ethnocentric Foundations of American Opinion* (Chicago: University of Chicago Press, 2009); and Howard Lavine, Milton Lodge, and Kate Freitas, "Threat, Authoritarianism, and Selective Exposure to Information," *Political Psychology* 26(2) (April 2005), 219–44.

41. John T. Jost, Jack Glaser, Arie W. Kruglanski, and Frank J. Sulloway, "Political Conservatism as Motivated Social Cognition," *Psychological Bulletin* 129 (3) (May 2003), 339–75.

42. This is the view of Lavine, Lodge, and Freitas, "Threat, Authoritarianism, and Selective Exposure to Information."

and laissez-faire conservatism is simply a commitment to free market principles.[43]

Defining Authoritarianism

There are as many variations on the definition of authoritarianism as there are scholars studying it. My definition of authoritarianism begins with Hetherington's recent explanation of it as "a distinct way of understanding political reality" that "shap[es] political behavior and identity."[44] To this I add Altemeyer's three-part description of what authoritarians do: Authoritarians submit to authority, prefer the conventional, and may act aggressively to those out-groups who question authority, are deemed unconventional, or both.[45] Then, to Altemeyer's foundation, I add four other aspects that are components of different contemporary characterizations of authoritarians.[46]

- First, authoritarian submission to authority is deeply rooted and compelled. Authoritarians follow authority because they seek order.[47] Authoritarians' need for order impels their submission to authority.

- Second, authoritarians' need for order compels them to act to defend it. When usurpers—through their actions or simply their existence—question, challenge, or seek to change an accepted order and norms, authoritarians rise aggressively to defend them.

43. While authoritarianism and racism are correlated in the United States, they are different. As Stenner notes, authoritarianism is an aversion to different "people and beliefs." Thus, the sources of authoritarian intolerance are much broader than race. *The Authoritarian Dynamic*, 150–154. Stenner's observation is quite important. It creates theoretical space for the empirically undeniable existence of left-wing authoritarian regimes, such as Hugo Chavez's government in Venezuela.

44. Hetherington and Weiler, *Authoritarianism and Polarization in American Politics*, 64.

45. Robert Altemeyer has written on the nature and characteristics of authoritarianism for most of his scholarly career. In addition to his 1981 work *Right-Wing Authoritarianism*, noted above, he has developed these lines of argument in *Enemies of Freedom: Understanding Right-Wing Authoritarianism* (San Francisco: Jossey–Bass, 1988); *The Authoritarian Specter* (Cambridge, Mass.: Harvard University Press, 1996); and *The Authoritarians* (published online: http://members.shaw.ca/jeanaltemeyer/drbob/TheAuthoritarians.pdf).

46. Matthew MacWilliams, "American Authoritarianism in Black and White."

47. Hetherington and Weiler, *Authoritarianism and Polarization in American Politics*, 33-34.

- Third, authoritarians' sense of order is not necessarily or solely defined by worldly powers. To authoritarians, there are higher powers that delineate right from wrong and good from evil. There are transcendent ways of behaving and being that are enduring, everlasting, and the root of balance and order.[48] These authorities are "morally and ontologically superior" to state or institutional authority and must be obeyed.[49] The higher authority may be otherworldly, or a text (for example, the Constitution) imbued with enlightened, transcendent power when its meaning is interpreted originally.

- Finally, I stipulate—as other students of authoritarianism have— that authoritarianism is universal and transcends society, culture, politics, and race. Authoritarianism is not limited to Europeans or whites. It does not discriminate. It is found in every culture and among members of every race.[50]

Authoritarianism and Threat

In all of its different manifestations and guises, threat is at the root of authoritarianism. It determines where an individual is likely to be located "on the continuum between authoritarian (closed) and democrat-

48. Stanley Feldman, "Values, Ideology, and the Structure of Political Attitudes," in *The Oxford Handbook of Political Psychology*, ed. David O. Sears, Leonie Huddy, and Robert Jervis (New York: Oxford University Press, 2003), 477–508.

49. Howard Gabennesch, "Authoritarianism as World View," *American Journal of Sociology* 77(5) (March 1972), 857–875.

50. This point can be found in, e.g., Adorno, et al., *The Authoritarian Personality*; Christie, "Authoritarianism Re-Examined"; Feldman and Stenner, "Perceived Threat and Authoritarianism"; Hetherington and Weiler, *Authoritarianism and Polarization in American Politics*; Stenner, *The Authoritarian Dynamic*; John J. Ray, "Half of all Authoritarians are Left Wing: A reply to Eyseneck and Stone," *Political Psychology* 4(1) (March 1983), 139–143; and Edward A. Shils, "Authoritarianism: Right and Left," in *Studies in the Scope and Method of "The Authoritarian Personality": Continuities in Social Research*, eds. Richard Christie and Marie Jahoda (Glencoe, Ill.: Free Press, 1954).

ic (open) beliefs";[51] as James Gibson has written, "threat perceptions are one of the strongest predictors of intolerance."[52]

Erich Fromm attributed Fascism's rise to threat. Isolated, powerless, and insecure people "escaped from freedom" by submitting to Nazi authoritarianism. Adorno et al.'s Freudian explanation of authoritarianism proposed that a threatening childhood environment created authoritarian adults. Rokeach argued that "adverse experiences, temporary or enduring," threaten individuals, create anxiety, and cause dogmatism and intolerance.[53] As such, over time, threat, uncertainty, and fear breed authoritarianism.[54]

A variety of threats have been theoretically implicated in authoritarianism and "point to threat as a primary, or perhaps as the primary, determinant of heightened authoritarianism."[55] Among them are personal threats; the threat of personal failure; threat aggregated and estimated across society; socially learned and experienced threats; external and internal fear and anxiety; intensely identified and conforming in-groups threatened by unconventional out-groups; individual and collective threats; personal insecurity caused by the threat of terrorism; and differentially perceived economic threats.[56]

---

51. Christian Welzel, "Individual Modernity," in *The Oxford Handbook of Political Behavior*, eds. Russell J. Dalton and Hans-Deiter Klingemann (Oxford: Oxford University Press, 2007), 189.

52. James L. Gibson, "Political Intolerance in the Context of Democratic Theory," in *The Oxford Handbook of Political Behavior*, 332.

53. Erich Fromm, *Escape from Freedom* (New York: Henry Holt and Company, 1941); Adorno et al., *The Authoritarian Personality*; Rokeach, *The Open and Closed Mind*, 69.

54. Many scholars have explored the relationship between threat, uncertainty, fear, and authoritarianism. In addition to the many works of Altemeyer noted above, major contributions include Samuel Fillenbaum and Arnold Jackman, "Dogmatism and Anxiety in Relation to Problem Solving: An Extension of Rokeach's Results," *Journal of Abnormal and Social Psychology* 63(1) (July 1961), 212–214; Seymour Martin Lipset, "Democracy and Working-Class Authoritarianism," *American Sociological Review* 24(4) (August 1959), 482–501; John J. Ray, "A New Balanced F Scale and its Relation to Social Class"; Nevitt Sanford, *Self and Society: Social Change and Individual Development* (New York: Atherton Press, 1966); and Glenn D. Wilson, *The Psychology of Conservatism* (New York: Academic Press, 1973).

55. Stephen M. Sales and Kenneth E. Friend, "Success and Failure as Determinants of Level of Authoritarianism," *Behavioral Science* 18(3) (May 1973), 163.

56. For the impact of personal threat on shaping authoritarian propensity, see Samuel Fillenbaum and Arnold Jackman, "Dogmatism and Anxiety in Relation to Problem Solving: An Extension of Rokeach's Results"; Lipset, *Political Man: The Social Bases of Politics*; and Sanford, *Self and Society: Social Change and Individual Development*. For the threat of

Nearly a half century after the publication of *The Authoritarian Personality*, however, the statistical evidence linking threat to authoritarianism remained sparse. Feldman and Stenner's work bridged this empirical gap.[57] Using childrearing questions included on the 1992 American National Election Studies (ANES) survey for the first time to estimate authoritarianism, they found, as one observer of the field has written, that "authoritarianism and perceptions of environmental stress [i.e., threat] interact in creating intolerance."[58] Threat did not make individuals more authoritarian. Instead, according to Feldman and Stenner's hypothesis, it activated intolerant authoritarian behaviors in individuals already predisposed to authoritarianism.

Feldman and Stenner's findings did not contradict the widely held assumption that long-term exposure to threat breeds authoritarianism. However, they challenge the notion that personal threats play an important role in authoritarianism. Feldman and Stenner contended that "[a]uthoritarianism is activated when there is a perception that the political or social order is threatened."[59] Based on their analysis of 1992 ANES data, threats to social norms and order from ideologically distant political parties or candidates, negatively perceived presidential

personal failure, see especially Sales and Friend, "Success and Failure as Determinants of Level of Authoritarianism." For aggregated threats and those estimated across society, see Stephen M. Sales, "Threat as a Factor in Authoritarianism: An Analysis of Archival Data," *Journal of Personality and Social Psychology* 28(1) (October 1973), 44–57. For socially learned and experienced threats, see the corpus of Altemeyer's work, particularly *Right-Wing Authoritarianism, Enemies of Freedom: Understanding Right-Wing Authoritarianism*, and *The Authoritarian Specter*. For the significance of both internal and external fear and anxiety, see Ray, "A New Balanced F Scale and Its Relation to Social Class," and Wilson, *The Psychology of Conservatism*. For in-group and out-group distinctions and their significance, see John Duckitt, "Authoritarianism and Group Identification: A New View of an Old Construct," *Political Psychology* 10(1) (March 1989), 63–84. For the salience of individual and collective threats, see Richard M. Doty, Bill E. Peterson, and David G. Winter, "Threat and Authoritarianism in the United States, 1978–1987," *Journal of Personality and Social Psychology* 61(4)(October 1991), 629–40. For the role of a sense of personal insecurity arising from terrorism, see Marc Hetherington and Elizabeth Suhay, "Authoritarianism, Threat, and Americans Support for the War on Terror," *American Journal of Political Science* 55(3) (July 2011), 546–560. On the differential perception of economic threats, see Lipset, "Democracy and Working-Class Authoritarianism"; and Sam G. McFarland and Vladimir S. Ageyev, "Economic Threat and Authoritarianism in the United States and Russia," paper presented at the annual meeting of the International Society for Political Psychology, Washington, D.C., 1995.

57. Feldman and Stenner, "Perceived Threat and Authoritarianism."

58. James L. Gibson, "Political Intolerance in the Context of Democratic Theory," 332.

59. Feldman and Stenner, "Perceived Threat and Authoritarianism," 765–66.

candidates, or a deteriorating national economy catalyze authoritarianism, while personal threats to individuals (for example, unemployment) do not.[60] The lack of a connection observed by Feldman and Stenner "[i]n the absence of threat…between authoritarian predispositions and the dependent variables"[61] also raised serious questions about the theoretical accounts forwarded both by Adorno and his co-authors and by Altemeyer of the origins of authoritarianism. To answer these questions, Feldman proposed, in a later article, a new explanation for authoritarianism that allows for the observed interactive effects of threat and authoritarianism. He posited that "authoritarian predispositions originate in the conflict between the values of social conformity and personal autonomy." When social conformity is threatened, authoritarian predispositions are activated and intolerant behavior is produced.[62]

Building on this work, Stenner proposed the "Authoritarian Dynamic," a "process in which an enduring individual predisposition interacts with changing environmental conditions—specifically, conditions of 'normative threat'—to produce manifest expressions of intolerance." There are three vitally important components of Stenner's theory. First, authoritarianism is conceptualized as an enduring predisposition that is partially inherited. Second, authoritarianism is not always evident; authoritarian behavior is activated "when needed." As such, "authoritarianism does not consistently predict behavior across different situations." Finally, not all threats are created equal. Only threats to norms and order, when they are perceived by an individual with an authoritarian predisposition, have the capacity to elicit an intolerant reaction.[63]

While Feldman and Stenner's account of the interaction between threats to moral order and authoritarianism is compelling and well documented, it is certainly not the last word. Other scholars found that threats to morality and mortality can activate authoritarian be-

<hr>

60 Ibid., 764. This is the first example of analysis of authoritarianism using childrearing questions that exclude all but whites from the data.

61.Ibid.,. 765.

62. Stanley Feldman, "Enforcing Social Conformity: A Theory of Authoritarianism," *Political Psychology* 24(1) (March 2003), 41, 51.

63. Stenner, *The Authoritarian Dynamic*, 13–14.

havior in individuals with a predisposition to authoritarianism. Using the Balanced F-scale to measure authoritarianism, Rickert found that authoritarians who were economically threatened were six times more likely "to favor restricting benefits to powerless groups" than authoritarians and nonauthoritarians who were not threatened.[64] Experimenting with situationally induced threats, Lavine et al. concluded that threats to cultural values as well as personal threats activate authoritarian behaviors in those predisposed to authoritarianism. Moreover, the experimental results implied "that authoritarians think and act as they do in order to reduce an apparently acute sensitivity to threat," an observation that is a half-step away from conceptualizing authoritarianism as a shield from threat.[65]

"Threats to social order and cohesion, social identity, economic security, and mortality" have all been associated with authoritarian activation.[66] Some scholars have argued that sociotropic threat (that is, a perceived threat to society) is a more important trigger of intolerant, antidemocratic behavior than personal threat.[67] By contrast, Darren Davis has contended that "when threat is personalized the response may become overwhelmingly intolerant toward perceived outgroups or threatening groups."[68] Thus, the list of scholars who find threats,

---

64. Edward J. Rickert, "Authoritarianism and Economic Threat: Implications for Political Behavior," *Political Psychology* 19(4) (December 1998), 707.

65. Howard Lavine, Milton Lodge, James Polichak, and Charles Taber. "Explicating the Black Box Through Experimentation: Studies of Authoritarianism and Threat," *Political Analysis* 10(4) (December 2001), 359. Greenberg et al. also contend authoritarians are more sensitive to threats to mortality than nonauthoritarians; see Jeff Greenberg, Tom Pyszczynski, Sheldon Solomon, Abram Rosenblatt, Mitchell Veeder, Shari Kirkland, and Deborah Lyon, "Evidence for Terror Management Theory II: The Effects of Mortality Salience on Reactions to Those Who Threaten or Bolster the Cultural Worldview," *Journal of Personality and Social Psychology* 58(2) (February 1990), 303-318.

66. Lavine, Lodge, and Freitas, "Threat, Authoritarianism, and Selective Exposure to Information," 227.

67. James Gibson, "A Sober Second Thought: An Experiment in Persuading Russians to Tolerate," *American Journal of Political Science* 42(3) (July 1998), 819–50; George E. Marcus, Elizabeth Theiss-Morse, John L. Sullivan, Sandra L. Wood, *With Malice Toward Some: How People Make Civil Liberties Judgments* (Cambridge. Cambridge University Press, 1995); John L. Sullivan, James Piereson, and George E. Marcus, *Political Tolerance and American Politics: The Empirical Literature* (Chicago: University of Chicago Press, 1993).

68. This quote summarizes some of the findings of Davis's paper on black political intolerance. Darren Davis, "Exploring Black Political Intolerance," *Political Behavior* 17(1) (March 1995), 1-22. The quote itself is taken from Darren Davis and Brian D. Silver, "Continuity and Change in Support for Civil Liberties after the 9/11 Terrorist

---

beyond threats to norms, are important triggers of authoritarianism is lengthy and distinguished: it includes Adorno, Altemeyer, Davis, Duckitt, Hetherington, Lavine, Lodge, Merolla, Oesterrich, Rickert, and Zechmeister. Who is activated by threat is as contested a question as what type of threat activates them. Many scholars take exception to Stenner's concept of an authoritarian dynamic and argue that authoritarian behavior is not turned on and off by the presence or absence of threat. To them the aggression that forms the bedrock of authoritarian behavior is chronically salient and not only influences how authoritarians act, but also persistently alters their perception of the world.[69] For example, Hetherington argues that authoritarians, perpetually in a state of hypervigilance, are always threatened and activated. Normative and physical threats do not further agitate their authoritarian predisposition; they are already acting or prepared to act. Instead, according to Hetherington and his coauthors, it is nonauthoritarians who, when confronting physical threats, act more like authoritarians.[70]

My own perspective on authoritarian activation is a hybrid of Stenner's authoritarian dynamic and Hetherington, Weiler, and Suhay's equally compelling observations. On the one hand, I hold that those Americans who are predisposed to authoritarianism are also more likely to feel threatened. When they perceive a mortal, physical threat or a moral, normative danger—which is, on balance, more often than the "average" American—their authoritarianism is activated. On the other hand, I contend that nonauthoritarians who perceive a mortal or moral threat will also become more aggressive and behave more like

Attacks: Results of a Panel Study," paper presented at the Annual Meeting of the American Political Science Association, 2003, 20; accessed at https://msu.edu/~bsilver/ContinuityAPSA2003.pdf.

69. This view is found in Adorno et al., *The Authoritarian Personality*, in the corpus of Altemeyer's works; in Hetherington and Weiler, *Authoritarianism and Polarization in American Politics*, Hetherington and Suhay, "Authoritarianism, Threat, and Americans' Support for the War on Terror"; and in Meloen, Van der Linden, and DeWitte, "A Test of the Approaches of Adorno et al., Lederer, and Altemeyer of Authoritarianism in Belgian Flanders."

70. Hetherington and Weiler, *Authoritarianism and Polarization in American Politics*, and Hetherington and Suhay, "Authoritarianism, Threat, and Americans' Support for the War on Terror."

authoritarians.[71] Thus, applying the cartoon character Pogo's well-known aphorism to nonauthoritarian Americans, "we have met the enemy, and he is us."

Measuring Authoritarianism

Measurement problems have plagued the study of authoritarianism since research on the question began. As noted above, the design and statistical validity of the first attempt to estimate individuals' innate predisposition to authoritarianism, the F-scale, was challenged just four years after its introduction. By the 1960s, many scholars considered the F-scale an "Edsel, a case study in how to do everything wrong."[72]

New measurement schemes also fell short of the measurement mark for a variety of reasons. For example, the Conservatism scale conflated authoritarianism with conservatism; the foundation of the Balanced F-scale remained the scientifically unfalsifiable Freudian psychodynamic theory; and while the Dogmatism scale avoided the conservative bias of both the Conservatism and F-scales, the questions comprising it were worded (like the F-Scale) in one direction and subject to acquiescent response bias.[73]

In an effort to resolve the ongoing authoritarian measurement problem, Altemeyer introduced the Right-Wing Authoritarian (RWA) scale in 1981 and has regularly updated it to reflect societal changes.[74] A number of scholars of the subject have recognized the RWA

71. Hetherington and Suhay make an important distinction between sociotropic physical threat and personal physical threat. They argue personal physical threat makes nonauthoritarians behave more like authoritarians. Sociotropic physical threat or, as operationalized in their study, perceiving "that the country is in danger" from terrorism (2011, 566) does not.

72. Alan Wolfe, "'The Authoritarian Personality' Revisited," *Chronicle of Higher Education* 52 (7) (October 7, 2005), B12. An excellent review of the genesis of the study of authoritarianism, the development of the F-scale, and the status of authoritarian theory and measurement is *Strengths and Weakness: The Authoritarian Personality Today*, ed. William F. Stone, Gerda Lederer, and Richard Christie (New York: Springer-Verlag, 1993).

73. John J. Ray, "The Development and Validation of a Balanced Dogmatism Scale," *Australian Journal of Psychology* 22(3) (December 1970), 253–60.

74. Altemeyer's RWA scale first appears in *Right-Wing Authoritarianism* (1981), and later updated and refined the scale in both *Enemies of Freedom: Understanding Right-Wing*

as an excellent tool for estimating authoritarian attitudes. Its fundamental strength is, however, its Achilles heel. Many of the questions on which the scale is based measure political attitudes. As such, the scale accurately measures authoritarian behavior, but does not identify individuals' underlying predisposition to authoritarianism.[75] This presents a particular theoretical problem for Stenner, who argues that authoritarianism is latent until activated by a normative threat. Since the RWA scale only measures an individual's expression of authoritarianism, it is liable to miss those authoritarians who are not (yet) activated at a particular point in time. To both Stenner and Hetherington the RWA scale is tautological—an excellent measurement of authoritarian prejudicial preferences but an inaccurate predictor of a predisposition to authoritarianism.[76]

The thicket of measurement problems intrinsic to the different scales designed to estimate authoritarianism consigned authoritarian studies to the "scholarly hinterlands" of political science for several decades.[77] That changed, however, when a new measure, based on four childrearing questions, appeared on the 1992 ANES survey. Questions about childrearing values had been used on the General Social Survey (GSS) since 1973 as a tool for estimating authoritarianism.[78] The inclusion of four similar questions on the ANES 1992 survey led to a revival of the study of authoritarianism by political scientists.

The childrearing questions appeared to resolve the vexing measurement problems that had bedeviled authoritarian scholars for decades. As Stenner succinctly explains, the four questions "enable us to distinguish authoritarian predisposition for authoritarian 'products' (attitudes)...which are sometimes manifested but sometimes not, and

Authoritarianism (1988) and *The Authoritarian Specter* (1996).

75. Hetherington and Weiler argue that the RWA scale "is so predictive of prejudice and intolerance... [because it is] largely a measure of prejudice and intolerance" and not authoritarianism. *Authoritarianism and Polarization in American Politics*, 47.

76. These commentaries and critiques are found in Feldman and Stenner, "Perceived Threat and Authoritarianism"; Stenner, *The Authoritarian Dynamic*; and Hetherington and Weiler, *Authoritarianism and Polarization in American Politics*.

77. As noted by Hetherington and Weiler, *Authoritarianism and Polarization in American Politics*, 36.

78. Julie Wronski, "Authoritarianism and Social Identity Sorting: Exploring the Sources of American Mass Partisanship," paper delivered at the National Capital Area Political Science Association American Politics Workshop, January 5, 2015.

whose specific content may vary across time and space."[79] Armed with a new tool for identifying authoritarians, political scientists pushed the study of authoritarianism back onto the scholarly agenda, starting with an analysis of data that examined the interaction of perceived threat and authoritarianism.[80]

Recently, however, concerns have been raised about the cross-racial validity of the four childrearing questions. Early analysis of these questions found a higher percentage of authoritarians among African Americans than among whites. This finding by itself invited greater scrutiny of the questions themselves and how they are understood within different communities. Two scholars, Efrén Pérez and Marc Hetherington, contend that the gap in the prevalence of authoritarianism between African Americans and whites produced when childrearing questions are asked is "largely a measurement artifact."[81] Put simply, they argue that African Americans and whites interpret the childrearing questions used to estimate authoritarianism differently—a difference that arises from their condition of being in groups characterized by very different relative positions of cultural power. Thus, while the two groups appear to be answering the same questions, their answers are based on different understandings of what the questions ask. The result, in Perez and Hetherington's view, is that the authoritarian scale generated by the childrearing questions is measuring different attitudes among whites than it is measuring among African Americans.

The cross-racial validity of the childrearing scale is an important question for any student of authoritarianism. Perez and Hetherington's argument for scale variance is based on theory and supported by evidence. The suggestion of a monolithic allegiance of African Americans to racial group identity, measured in surveys through linked-fate questions, is pointed to as a root cause of variant interpretations of the childrearing questions among blacks.[82] The different

79. Stenner, *The Authoritarian Dynamic*, 24.

80. Feldman and Stenner, "Perceived Threat and Authoritarianisms."

81. Efrén O. Pérez and Marc J. Hetherington, "Authoritarianism in Black and White: Testing the Cross-Racial Validity of the Child Rearing Scale," *Political Analysis* 22(3) (Summer 2014), 399.

82. The linked-fate approach to understanding distinctive attitudes within racial groups is discussed in Katherine Tate, *From Protest to Politics: The New Black Voters in American*

attitudes expressed by black and white American authoritarians on issues surveyed in two polls (the 2008 ANES and the 2010 YouGov Polimetrix survey), which should theoretically engage respondents' authoritarian predispositions, adds evidentiary weight to Pérez and Hetherington's hypothesis. But it is the finding of statistical variance between black and white Americans in their understanding of childrearing questions asked on the 2008 ANES that provides Perez and Hetherington's theory with empirical heft.[83]

The question of the childrearing scale's validity across races is not a settled issue. To explore the issue of scale's validity in more detail, I tested childrearing questions from five national polls in addition to the 2008 ANES.[84] I found support for Perez and Hetherington's theory that responses to authoritarian questions are variant between black and white Americans in one additional survey. But on the other four surveys examined, a multi-group confirmatory factor analysis found that the responses were invariant between the two groups. In other words, on four surveys, black and white Americans' understandings of the childrearing questions were statistically similar—which means the authoritarian scale derived from the questions was valid across racial differences.[85]

Interestingly, the two surveys in which responses to authoritarian questions varied included "both" as an answer in addition to the paired childrearing responses. The four surveys in which the responses were invariant—and, therefore, valid—did not offer "both" as a response. The theoretical argument here is that the authoritarian scale will be invariant and valid for black and white Americans when responses to the childrearing questions are limited to paired attributes—and sur-

Elections (Cambridge, Mass.: Harvard University Press, 1994); and Michael Dawson, *Behind the Mule: Race and Class in African–American Politics* (Princeton: Princeton University Press, 1994).

83. Pérez and Hetherington, "Authoritarianism in Black and White," 402–04.

84. Polls analyzed include: the 2008, 2011, and 2012 American National Election Studies surveys; the 2008 AmericasBarometer Survey; the 2014 University of Massachusetts module on the Cooperative Congressional Election Study; and a December 2015 study I conducted under the auspices of the University of Massachusetts.

85. My findings are detailed in MacWilliams, "American Authoritarianism in Black and White."

vey respondents are not offered the option of choosing "both" as an answer.[86]

The upshot here is that the scale derived from the childrearing questions is still a good measurement of authoritarianism. And the scale's questions also provide a scientifically unbiased tool for estimating authoritarian support for Donald Trump—and assessing whether American authoritarians are more likely to favor him over other Republican candidates for president.

In light of the racially charged nature of Trump's campaign—and the very different perspectives toward his candidacy of different racial groups—this point demands some further exploration. The political behavior of many African Americans is typically caught in a tug of war between their racial identity and whatever predisposition to authoritarianism they might feel. When an issue at hand engages the authoritarian predispositions of African Americans, authoritarianism can trump racial identity—producing attitudes that defy conventional wisdom, and dashing the common (and wrong) theoretical assumption in political science that African American political behavior is homogeneous. When it comes to the candidacy of Donald Trump, however, African Americans' racial identity and historic partisan identity will overwhelm any disposition to authoritarianism. Since the 1948 executive orders of President Truman that desegregated the military and banned raced-based discrimination in federal hiring, a majority of African American have identified as Democrats. African American general election support for Republican presidential candidates has dwindled ever since, with only Eisenhower in 1956 (39 percent) and Nixon in 1960 (32 percent) the last Republican candidates to receive more than 30 percent of the African American vote. Even so, Trump's ascriptive candidacy may set a new low watermark for African American support of Republican presidential candidates.

---

86. The statistical similarities between white and African American groups on two worldview principles and a range of worldview evolution issues—are further developed in MacWilliams, "American Authoritarianism in Black and White."

Measuring American Authoritarians' Support for Donald Trump

To test the hypothesis that Trump's unvarnished, us-versus-them message and bellicose manner activated American authoritarians and drove them to rally behind him, I fielded a national public opinion survey. The poll was conducted online in December of 2015, approximately one month before the opening nominating contests in Iowa and New Hampshire. It sampled 1,800 registered voters.[87] The topline results of the survey compared quite favorably to the findings of the *New York Times* poll fielded during roughly the same period.[88]

Using the childrearing battery of questions to estimate authoritarianism, the national poll found that authoritarianism was one of only two variables that were statistically and substantively significant predictors of Trump support among likely Republican primary voters. Of course, many other theories have been advanced to explain Trump's rise. Byrd and Collingwood argue racial resentment is behind Trump's rise.[89] Clifford Young of Ipsos points to nativism.[90] Rahn and Oliver contend economic populism is behind Trump's success.[91] Following Hetherington and Weiler, I stipulate that authoritarianism is a predisposition that arises causally *prior* to the political attitudes and behavior that it affects.[92] As such, it occurs before ideology, partisan-

---

87. The survey included standard demographic questions, feeling thermometers on political figures, groups of people, and organizations, screens to identify likely primary and general voters, candidate preference questions, items assessing respondents' worries about the sociotropic and personal threats posed by terrorism, and a bevy of values and policy questions. The Republican survey population was 558, which included eighteen African Americans.

88. The *New York Times* poll was a landline and cell survey that came out of the field one week before my online poll. It pegged Trump's vote at 35 percent. My survey reported Trump's support at 34.5 percent.

89. Daniel Byrd and Loren Collingwood, "Bernie Sanders: Lifting Up the Masses or the Few?" TeleSUR, http://www.telesurtv.net/english/opinion/Bernie-Sanders-Lifting-up-the-Masses-or-the-Few--20160331-0068.html, accessed August 12, 2016.

90. Clifford Young, "It's Nativism: Explaining the Drivers of Trump's Popular Support," *Ipsos Ideas Spotlight*, June 1, 2016, http://spotlight.ipsos-na.com/index.php/news/its-nativism-explaining-the-drivers-of-trumps-popular-support/ , accessed August 12, 2016.

91. Wendy Rahn and Eric Oliver, "Trump's voters aren't authoritarians, new research says. So what are they?," *Washington Post*, March 9, 2015, https://www.washingtonpost.com/news/monkey-cage/wp/2016/03/09/trumps-voters-arent-authoritarians-new-research-says-so-what-are-they/ .

92. Hetherington and Weiler, *Authoritarianism and Polarization in American Politics*, 145.

ship, and the other "isms" that have been offered to explain Trump's rise. The authoritarian inclination of Trump voters are abundantly clear when the predicted probability of supporting Trump is estimated and arrayed across the authoritarian scale (Figure 1).[93]

The only other variable that was statistically significant was personal fear of terrorism.[94] Additional variables in the regression model included sex, educational attainment, age, church attendance, evangelicalism, ideology, race, and income—all are typically reliable predictors of support for or opposition to a candidate. These variables had

Figure 1:
Predicted support for Trump among likely Republican voters
by degree of authoritarianism

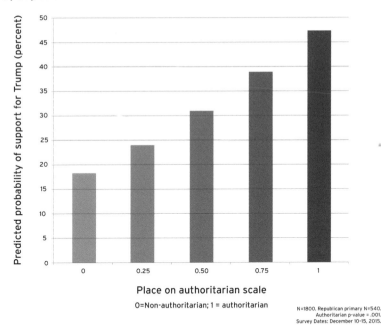

Place on authoritarian scale
0=Non-authoritarian; 1 = authoritarian

N=1800. Republican primary N=540.
Authoritarian p-value = .001.
Survey Dates: December 10-15, 2015.

---

93. The 95 percent confidence intervals range from .0661 to .2997 for nonauthoritarians (0) to .3416 to .6051 for authoritarians (1).

94. The wording of this question is: "How worried are you that you or someone in your family will become a victim of terrorism?" Question answers ranged from "Not At All" to "A Lot" on a 7-point Likert scale.

no statistical bearing on support for Trump (Appendix, Table 1).[95] Importantly, when it comes to authoritarianism, Trump supporters were also distinct in their attitudes from the followers of other Republican candidates for president. Support models for Ted Cruz, Ben Carson, Marco Rubio, and Jeb Bush, estimated using the same set of independent variables, found that authoritarianism had no effect on support for Trump's opponents (Appendix, Table 2).

The difference between predicted authoritarian support for Trump and for all other Republican candidates is readily apparent when combined into one chart (Figure 2). Looking at this figure, it is important to note that authoritarianism is only a statistically significant variable

Figure 2:
Percent probability of supporting alternative candidates among likely Republican primary voters, by degree of authoritarianism

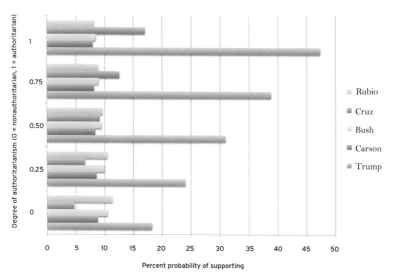

for Trump. Thus, while the difference between the predicted value of Trump's support among authoritarians and nonauthoritarians is sta-

95. I reluctantly included many of these tag-along independent variables to preempt potential objections that the model was tweaked to make authoritarianism statistically and substantively significant. Of course, including these variables creates another potential statistical problem—collinearity. In the model as specified, I did not find a collinearity problem that would change the finding of the importance of authoritarianism to Donald Trump's support.

tistically meaningful, any variation in support across the authoritarian scale for the other candidates is not.

The Role of Fear and Authoritarianism in Trump's Rise

As discussed earlier, while scholars differ on the specific origin of authoritarianism, threat and fear have long been theorized to play an important role in the activation of authoritarian behavior and the expression of authoritarian attitudes. Indeed, the linkage between threat and authoritarian behavior has remained a central focus of authoritarian studies from more than seven decades. Hetherington, Weiler, and Suhay have all advanced what I call the Pogo principle—that "[a]s people in the middle and lower tiers of authoritarianism come to perceive threat, they adopt policy orientations that are more like an authoritarian's."[96]

With the terrorist attacks in Paris in mid-November of 2015 and the San Bernardino terrorist shootings occurring just two weeks later, I expected that fear of terrorism was rising—and that polling would find those who were more worried about terrorism would be more likely to support Trump. Theoretically, authoritarians and nonauthoritarians who are more worried about terrorism should be a receptive audience for the finger-pointing of a fear mongering candidate like Donald Trump.

The results from the national survey I conducted provided empirical support for this hypothesis, finding that personal fear of terrorism was a statistically significant predictor of support for Trump. Activated authoritarians, as well as fearful Americans, were (and remain) key components of Trump's base. Trump's calls for vigilance hit home with activated authoritarians as well as with an audience of nonauthoritarians primed by fear.

Graphed once again using predicted probabilities, the effect of fear of terrorism on support for Trump among less authoritarian voters is unmistakable. The more fearful nonauthoritarians are of the threat posed by terrorism, the more likely they are to support Donald Trump (Figure 3). Comparing those who are not at all afraid of terrorism to

96. Hetherington and Weiler, *Authoritarianism and Polarization in American Politics*, 113.

Figure 3:
Support for Trump among likely Republican voters
by degree of authoritarianism and fear of terrorism

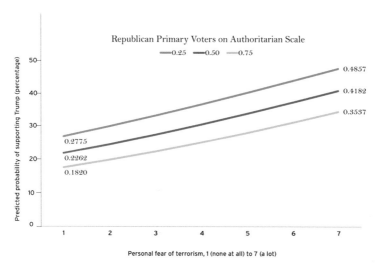

those who fear terrorism a lot, the effect of fear on support for Trump is statistically significant at a confidence interval of 95 percent.

How Do We Know That Trump Supporters Are Authoritarians?

A common objection raised by skeptics of the four-question authoritarian scale is that the childrearing qualities it measures are not accurate estimators of an individual's disposition to authoritarianism. One simple way to test this objection and answer skeptics is to assess whether Trump voters express authoritarian attitudes. In other words, if Trump voters really are authoritarians, more often than not they should behave like authoritarians. Not only should they walk like a duck (by testing dispositionally authoritarian); they also should talk like a duck (by expressing authoritarian attitudes on a wide range of issues). In short, they are authoritarian walkers and talkers.

Several questions in the national survey were designed to test for authoritarian behavior. These questions spring from a robust literature that dates back to Fromm's aptly named 1941 study Escape From Freedom, spans seven decades, and abundantly details authoritarians' fear of "the other," antipathy for the ideals of Madisonian democracy, and disdain for the protection of minority rights from majority tyranny. As such, the questions probe survey respondents' attitudes toward bedrock Democratic values that are the foundation of constitutional government and civil society.

On most of these questions, Trump voters exhibit statistically significant and substantive authoritarian attitudes (Figure 4). For example, Trump voters are statistically more likely to agree that "other groups" should sometimes be kept in their place. And they support preventing minority opposition once "we decide" what is right.[97]

Trump supporters kick the fundamental tenets of Madisonian democracy to the curb, asserting that the rights of minorities need not be protected from the power of the majority. And they are statistically more likely than Trump opponents to agree the president should curtail the voice and vote of the opposition when it is necessary to protect

Figure 4: Attitudes of Trump voters on questions of democratic principles

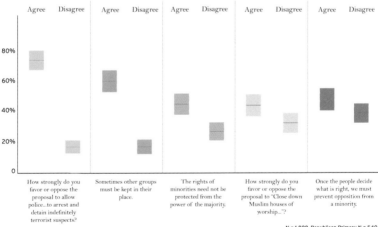

N = 1,800. Republican Primary N = 540.
Trump voter p-values < .05 on all questions.
Survey Dates: 10 – 15 December 2015.

---

97. The wording of these questions is: "Sometimes other groups must be kept in their place" and "Once the people decide what is right, we must prevent opposition from a minority." Question answers ranged from "Strongly Disagree" to "Strongly Agree" on a 7-point Likert scale.

the country—although a plurality still opposes this constitutionally questionable exercise of presidential power.[98]

Trump voters are also ready to suspend the constitutionally protected Writ of Habeas Corpus by empowering police and law enforcement to arrest and detain indefinitely anyone in the United States suspected of belonging to a terrorist organization. And Trump supporters agree that mosques across the United States should be closed down—a clear abridgment of the religious freedoms guaranteed in the First Amendment of the Bill of Rights.[99]

A majority of Republican authoritarians in my poll also strongly supported Trump's proposals to deport 11 million illegal immigrants, prohibit Muslims from entering the United States, and establish a nationwide database to track Muslims in America, whether they are citizens or not. By comparison, on all of these questions, the attitudes of Cruz, Carson, Rubio, and Bush supporters are statistically insignificant. Hence, supporters of Trump express authoritarian attitudes on a wide range of important questions, while supporters of his erstwhile Republican opponents did not.

Trump 2016: Anomalous Outlier or Political Turning Point?

Like Trump's us-versus-them rhetoric, authoritarian voters are not new to America. Authoritarianism is a disposition that knows no geographic, racial, political, or societal boundaries; Americans are not immune from it. As the ascriptive tradition runs deep through American development, the disposition to authoritarianism, at least as measured since 1992 by means of childrearing questions, is a stable fixture within the American electorate. And the paranoid style of politics has been

---

98. The wording of this question is: "If it is necessary to protect our country, the president should limit the voice and vote of opposition parties." Question answers ranged from "Strongly Disagree" to "Strongly Agree" on a 7-point Likert scale. This question is not displayed in Figure 4.

99. The wording of these questions is: "How strongly do you favor or oppose the proposal to allow police and other law enforcement agencies to arrest and detain indefinitely anyone in the United States who is suspected of belonging to a terrorist organization?" and, "How strongly do you favor or oppose the proposal to 'Close down Muslim houses of worship—known as mosques—across the United States'?" Question answers ranged from "Strongly Favor" to "Strongly Oppose" on a 7-point Likert scale.

mined by politicians from Andrew Jackson to Pat Buchanan to activate that disposition.

But Trump's success, his dispatch of the Republican establishment and hostile takeover of the Republican Party, is a singular, unique achievement of the paranoid style and ascriptive tradition in contemporary American politics. Why was 2016 different from the nominating contests that have preceded it? What conditions made the 2016 nominating campaign ripe for the rise of an authoritarian candidate like Trump? And, importantly, is 2016 a harbinger of a new rising challenge to America's liberal and republican traditions? Or is Trump's triumph a "black swan"—an outlier with undoubtedly important ramifications but still a singular moment?

My poll shows empirically that American authoritarian voters responded to Trump's siren call, making him their first and only candidate of choice. The steadfast support of these authoritarian voters, combined with the support of fear-filled nonauthoritarians, provided a virtually unassailable foundation for Trump's candidacy. But the survey does not answer the deeper question: Why was this enough to win the Republican nomination in 2016?

While activating American authoritarians and catalyzing support among fearful voters were both necessary conditions for Trump to wage a competitive campaign for the Republican presidential nomination, I submit that they were not sufficient to produce his victory. A confluence of eight additional factors, unique to the 2016 Republican nomination contest, aided and abetted Trump's rise and secured his nomination. These eight factors are:

- The historically large field of primary candidates vying for the nomination.
- The failure of party elites.
- The sorting of authoritarians into the Republican Party.
- Rising public concern about terrorism, reinforced by terrorism incidents that took place during the nominating contest.
- A transformed media landscape.
- The delegitimization of institutions and leaders.
- The normative threats posed by recognized demographic changes in the United States.

- The celebrity and media acumen of the candidate himself.

Only one of these eight factors—the last—is specific to Trump. The others are features of the political landscape, independent of Trump's candidacy. For better or worse, many of them are likely to be persistent elements of the political landscape for years to come, providing fertile ground for the campaigns of ascriptive candidates who are likely to follow Trump's example. As such, examining the seven-layered petri dish of nutrients that nourished and sustained Trump's candidacy throughout the nominating process is important not only to understand the rise of Trump, but also to identify the potential for future ascriptive candidacies.

Let us start at the top of the list with the surfeit of candidates running for the nomination.

1. Historically Large Field of Candidates

Beginning on March 23, 2015, with Senator Ted Cruz's announcement, a total of 17 major candidates ran for the Republican nomination for president.[100] This was the largest number of candidates ever to have competed for the nomination, surpassing the previous record of 15 competitors in the 1948 election. The plethora of contenders in 2016, their breadth of experience, and their differing appeal to varying factions of the party fragmented the GOP primary electorate and effectively lowered the number of votes needed to win in the initial caucuses and primaries, opening the door for a Trump candidacy.

2. Failure of Party Elites

Leading scholars of American politics argue that political party insiders, defined quite broadly, exert considerable influence over the presidential nomination process of both parties. Starting with "invisible primaries" the "candidates put themselves forward, but the party coalition chooses among them, now as in the past."[101]

In 2016, the party elites failed to choose a preferred candidate during the invisible primary phase of the nominating contest and, as the actual caucuses and primaries ensued, coalesced only in opposition

---

100. Seventeen is the number of announced, mainstream candidates. Other fringe candidates also ran for the Republican nomination. For example, twenty-six candidates appeared on the New Hampshire Republican presidential primary ballot.

101. Cohen, Karol, Noel, and Zaller, *The Party Decides*, 11.

to Trump and not in support of one alternative to him. The division among party elites and the unity among Trump's authoritarian supporters provided his candidacy with the opportunity to win early contests and build electoral momentum. *Veni, vidi, vici* is a much simpler task to perform when the opposition is internally divided. Trump did not need to divide and conquer; he only needed to conquer.

3. Authoritarian Sorting

The slow but steady movement of authoritarians to the Republican Party over the last several decades, coupled with the splintering of the Republican primary vote, may have created a tipping point in 2016 in which the number of authoritarians identifying as Republicans was finally large enough, if activated, to win a significant number of primary and caucuses as well as the nomination.

Hetherington and Weiler have demonstrated that authoritarianism is behind the increasing partisan polarization in America. They have shown that "a coalitional reconfiguration of the parties is in the works, with authoritarians increasingly gravitating toward the Republican Party and nonauthoritarians increasingly gravitating toward the Democratic."[102] The data Hetherington and Weiler use to develop their partisan transformation hypothesis is based on cross sectional data from four surveys, with the fourth and final survey—conducted by ANES in 2006—providing the critical evidence in support of the argument.[103] But, as Hetherington and Weiler dutifully warn (twice) in their discussion of this data, only half of survey respondents in

---

102. Hetherington and Weiler, *Authoritarianism and Polarization in American Politics*, 158. The mechanism behind the partisan reconfiguration hypothesized by Hetherington and Weiler is an extension of the "issues evolution" process in which dormant issues increase in salience and persist over time, creating new lines of cleavage between parties. The evolution of these issues as important markers of partisan differences slowly but surely cause some voters to shift allegiances to the party more aligned with their issue interests. Hetherington and Weiler assert that as more new issues arise and are organically added to the issues separating parties, an issues evolution can morph into a worldview evolution. The recent transformation from an issues to a worldview evolution began with the addition of gut-level issues to the political debate. These gut-level, Cultural War concerns that elites have added to the issue agenda since the 1960s, drove the existing wedge between authoritarians and nonauthoritarians deeper—expanding, sharpening, and calcifying a new cleavage line that first formed at the beginning of the issues evolution. The result is the sorting of authoritarians over time into the Republican Party.

103. This is the 2006 ANES Pilot Study. This study reinterviewed 675 people from the 2004 ANES. Only half of the 2006 sample was asked a partisan identification question. See Hetherington and Weiler, *Authoritarianism and Polarization in American Politics*, 174.

the 2006 ANES were asked a partisanship question, raising possible questions about the certainty of their findings.

To explore the role of authoritarianism in partisan sorting in more depth, I pooled data from the 1992, 2000, 2004, 2008, and 2012 ANES surveys.[104] This increased the time frame of Hetherington and Weiler's partisanship examination by six years and yielded a robust sample of 8,549 individuals when African Americans were excluded, and 10,925 when African Americans were included.[105]

I find that when African Americans are excluded from the sample, the interaction term between authoritarianism and the survey year is positive and statistically significant, meaning that authoritarianism had an effect on partisanship during the twenty years studied. When African Americans are included in the analysis, the interaction term between authoritarian and survey year remains positive and statistically significant. These findings bolster Hetherington and Weiler's hypothesis that authoritarians have been steadily changing their partisan identification and sorting themselves into the Republican Party.[106]

4. Rising Public Concerns Over Terrorism

The terrorist attacks in Paris on November 13, 2015, and in San Bernardino, California just two weeks later (on December 2), reinforced existing public concerns about the threat terrorism poses to Americans and their families. Since mid-2008, Gallup has documented a rising fear among Americans that they or someone in their family "will become a victim of terrorism."[107] In 2008, 38 percent of Americans admitted they were very worried or somewhat worried about this possibility. By 2015, before the Paris and San Bernardino attacks, over half of all Americans (51 percent) were concerned about becoming a terrorist victim—the second highest level of concern registered in al-

---

104. The partial sample from the 2006 ANES survey (N=249) is not included in the pooled data.

105. Hetherington and Weiler's analysis is based on a sample from which African Americans were excluded. I ran an analysis without African American to replicate their work and one with African Americans to assess authoritarian sorting across the electorate.

106. While significant, the authoritarian effect on partisanship found in both cases is less than what was observed by Hetherington and Weiler.

107. Justin McCarthy, "Trust in Government to Protect Against Terrorism at New Low," Gallup, December 11, 2015, http://www.gallup.com/poll/187622/trust-government-protect-against-terrorism-new-low.aspx.

most 30 years of tracking by Gallup.[108] In the same poll taken in early December of 2015, two of every three Americans (67 percent) agreed that acts of terrorism in the United States were very or somewhat likely to occur in the next few weeks, a rise of 22 percentage points in just six months. Contemporaneously, confidence in the ability of the U.S. government to protect Americans from terrorism fell to the lowest point since 9/11.[109]

Growing fear of the terrorist threat primed authoritarian receptivity to Trump's message and, following Hetherington's negative interaction theory, made nonauthoritarians who were concerned about terrorist threats more likely to support Trump.[110] In short, a rising tide of fear lifted Trump's electoral yacht while swamping the boats of candidates like Ben Carson—who did not play the fear card as well, or as consistently, as Trump—and Jeb Bush, who refused to play the fear card on terrorism or immigration. In fact, Bush's August 2015 defense of his quote that immigration was "an act of love"[111]—and Trump's subsequent public mockery and "chilling attack" on the statement[112]—did irreparable damage to Bush's candidacy and helped seal his long, slow demise.[113]

---

108. Only during the period immediately following the 9/11 attacks have Americans expressed more concern about becoming a victim of terrorism. Ibid.

109. Ibid.

110. Hetherington and Weiler's theory (found also in the later work of Hetherington and Suhay) is that nonauthoritarians behave more like authoritarians when they feel threatened. Hetherington et al. argue that since authoritarianism is "always on," authoritarianians have nowhere to move on an attitudinal scale when they feel threatened. Instead it is the nonauthoritarians who, in moving toward authoritarian views and votes under conditions of threat, increase the significance and salience of this strand in overall political discourse. (This is the "Pogo effect" discussed above.) Karen Stenner, on the other hand, argues that authoritarianism is activated by threat—and, specifically, threat to norms. Otherwise, she holds, it is dormant. See Marc Hetherington and Jonathan Weiler, *Authoritarianism and Polarization in American Politics*, 113–15; Marc Hetherington and Elizabeth Suhay, "Authoritarianism, Threat, and American's Support for the War on Terror"; and Karen Stenner, *The Authoritarian Dynamic*.

111. Rebecca Shabad, "Jeb Bush stands by 'act of love' remark on illegal immigration," *The Hill*, August 6, 2015, http://thehill.com/blogs/ballot-box/presidential-races/250505-jeb-defends-act-of-love-immigration-comment.

112. Trump used the murder of Kathryn Steinle in San Francisco by an illegal immigrant to bludgeon Jeb Bush and demonstrate the inability of the government to protect Americans from "the other."

113. Philip Ricker, "Chilling Trump video attacks Bush for calling illegal immigration 'act of love'" *The Washington Post*, August 31, 2015, https://

5. *The Demographic Transformation of America*

In September of 2015 the Pew Research Center updated its projections on the changing demographics of the United States, reporting that "50 years after passage of the landmark law that rewrote U.S. immigration policy, nearly 59 million immigrants have arrived in the United States."[114] A later report, released in January of 2016, concludes that "[t]he U.S. is on its way to becoming a majority nonwhite nation."[115]

The growing diversity of America and the impending minority status of whites is not news. Neither is the alarmist response to it by American nativists. In 2006, in his hyperbolically titled book *State of Emergency: The World Invasion and Conquest of America*, Pat Buchanan, the twice-defeated candidate for the Republican nomination for president, once again warned that immigration and increasing racial diversity threatens the very fabric of America and could lead to anarchy.[116] In an NPR interview conducted in May of 2016, Buchanan, Trump's political predecessor, averred that "we're about—what?—25 years away from the fact where Americans of European descent will be a minority in the United States…. Now in half the homes in California, people speak a language other than English in their own homes. Anybody that believes that a country can be maintained that has no ethnic core to it or no linguistic core to it, I believe, is naïve in the extreme."[117]

Trump's call to build a wall and deport 11 million "illegals," his labeling of Mexican immigrants as rapists and murders, and his defin-

www.washingtonpost.com/news/post-politics/wp/2015/08/31/
chilling-trump-video-attacks-bush-for-calling-illegal-immigration-act-of-love/.

114. Pew Research Center, "Modern Immigration Wave Brings 59 Million to U.S.,
Driving Population Growth and Change Through 2065," September 28, 2015, http://
www.pewhispanic.org/2015/09/28/modern-immigration-wave-brings-59-million-to-u-s-
driving-population-growth-and-change-through-2065/.

115. Paul Taylor, "The demographic trends shaping American politics in 2016 and
beyond," Pew Research Center, January 27, 2016, http://www.pewresearch.org/
fact-tank/2016/01/27/the-demographic-trends-shaping-american-politics-in-2016-and-
beyond/.

116. Patrick J. Buchanan, *State of Emergency: The Third World Invasion and Conquest of
America* (New York: St. Martin's Press, 2006).

117. Pat Buchanan, interview by Rachel Martin, "Pat Buchanan On Why He Shares
Trump's Ideas on Foreign Policy," NPR, May 5, 2016, transcript,
http://www.npr.org/2016/05/05/476844409/
pat-buchanan-on-why-he-shares-trump-s-ideas-on-foreign-policy.

ing of Latinos and Muslims as "the other" connects with the concerns of American nativists led by Buchanan—those Americans who fear diversity and want to turn back the demographic clock to 1960 when, in Buchanan's reverie, we had "a really united country where 97 percent of us spoke English" and whites were in a hegemonic majority.[118] Buchanan and Trump's clarion call to these Americans of the ascriptive tradition are even more potent now, as the end of white hegemony in America approaches.

6. Transformed Media Landscape

The unparalleled style of Donald Trump's primary campaign, characterized by commentators as a "bizarre spectacle" from his announcement onward,[119]made for magnetic, must-see media that drew eyeballs, drove ratings, and, for legacy broadcast and cable news media operations, generated much-needed revenue. An early indication of what was to come came in September of 2015, when CNN was able to raise its advertising rates for one thirty-second spot in the second debate between Republican candidates from $5,000 to $200,000.[120] Advertising rates across cable news channels rose throughout the fall of 2015 and well into the spring of 2016 as a symbiotic relationship between Trump and the media developed. Trump provided well-timed and compelling content, and the media obligingly covered it. Trump rallies were timed to maximize live coverage. Trump tweets were geared to shape the media narrative, or change it to his liking.

All campaigns seek to shape and drive the media narrative to their advantage, but Trump's manipulation of the media was unrivaled. The content he offered may have been thin, but the style in which his pronouncements erupted proved irresistible to attention-hungry media outlets—leaving the milquetoast pronouncements of his opponents overwhelmed and forgotten. Gripped by the political reality show that was unpredictably unfolding before them, Americans rubbernecked their way through the nominating process. The media covered Trump incessantly. Media ratings and revenue increased. And Trump's campaign vaulted to the top of national polls of Republican voters, first

118. Ibid.

119. Adam Lerner, "The 10 best lines from Donald Trump's announcement speech."

120. Michael Addady, "CNN boosts ad rates for debate – Trump claims credit," *Fortune*, September 6, 2015, http://fortune.com/2015/09/06/trump-cnn-ad/.

rising to the top on July 15, 2015—and never being significantly challenged for the balance of the nominating contest.

Trump's dominance of the media from his announcement on is as stunning (Figure 5) as his unchallenged dominance in national polling is remarkable.

The legacy media followed the money—not so much the money Trump spent on advertising (which was negligible), but the money generated by the growing ratings associated with covering the spectacle of his campaign. In doing so, it amplified and mainstreamed Trump's authoritarian, us-versus-them message and American authoritarians answered. But mass media was not the only communication tool employed by Trump. As Steve Case noted in an email quoted in the *New York Times*, "Trump leveraged a perfect storm. A combo of social media (big following), brand (celebrity figure), creativity (pithy tweets), speed/timeliness (dominating news cycles)."[121] With over sev-

Figure 5:
Value of media coverage of Republican candidates,
by paid-media equivalent dollars

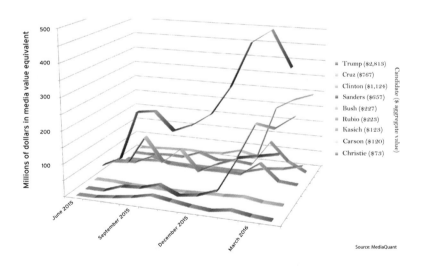

Source: MediaQuant

---

121. Patrick Healy and Jonathan Martin, "Republican Party Unravels Over Donald Trump's Takeover, *New York Times*, May 7, 2016, http://www.nytimes.com/2016/05/08/us/politics/republican-party-unravels-over-donald-trumps-takeover.html. Steve Case is the founder of AOL.

en million followers on Twitter and Facebook, Trump used the social media platforms of the Arab Spring to cyber-bully critics, savage opponents, threaten violence—and foment America's Authoritarian Spring.[122]

Trump fused mass rally demonstrations of unity and power, the immediacy and unfiltered messaging of social media, and the revenue needs of legacy media to construct a twenty-first century, strongman megaphone never before seen in politics. Wielding this instrument Trump galvanized supporters, gutted the opposition, and dominated the media narrative. Lamenting the death of liberalism and ascendance of authoritarianism in the United States and around the globe, Richard Cohen averred that "nationalism and authoritarianism, reinforced by technology, have come together to exercise new forms of control and manipulation over human beings."[123] Trump has proven himself an adept user of new media and a master manipulator of legacy media.

7. Delegitimized Institutions and Leaders

While fear of the threat posed by terrorism rose to historic levels and coverage of Trump's pugilistic message and manner dominated the media, Americans' confidence and trust in institutions and traditional leadership reached new lows in 2015, creating a receptive and ready environment for Trump's caustic, fear-laden, and anti-establishment message.

In its November 2015 report "Beyond Distrust: How Americans View Their Government," the Pew Research Center documented how toxic Americans' perceptions of their leaders and institution had become. Americans' trust in their government was "at historically low levels," with just 19 percent agreeing they trusted "the federal gov-

---

122. By May 2016, Trump's followers on Twitter and Facebook surpassed 8 million. For his adroit use of social media to achieve these objectives, see Alexander Burns and Maggie Haberman, "To Fight Critics, Donald Trump Aims to Instill Fear in 140-Character Doses," *New York Times*, February 26, 2016, http http://www.nytimes.com/2016/02/27/us/politics/donald-trump.html; Nick Gass, "Trump unleashes Facebook, Twitter war on Rubio," Politico, March 7, 2016, http://www.politico.com/story/2016/03/trump-slams-marco-rubio-social-media-220374; Jon Queally, "'It's Not a Threat!': Trump Says He'll Order Supporters to Disrupt Sanders' Rallies," *Common Dreams*, March 13, 2016, http://www.commondreams.org/news/2016/03/13/its-not-threat-trump-says-hell-order-supporters-disrupt-sanders-rallies.

123. Roger Cohen, "The Death of Liberalism," *New York Times*, April 14, 2016, http://www.nytimes.com/2016/04/14/opinion/the-death-of-liberalism.html.

ernment to do what is right just about always (3 percent) or most of the time (16 percent)." The percentage of Americans who think the government is "run for the benefit of all people" also stood at 19 percent—a 45-percentage point decline since 1964. Among registered voters, 27 percent "say they think of the government as an enemy," including 35 percent of Republicans and 34 percent of Independents, up 22 and 13 percentage points respectively since 1996. More than two of three Americans (68 percent) say the federal government does a "very bad" or "somewhat bad" job of managing immigration, creating a wide opening for Trump's immigration critique. Slightly fewer than three of every four Americans (74 percent) agree that "elected officials don't care about people like me." And exactly three of four Americans (75 percent) think corruption is "widespread throughout the government in this country."[124] About the same percent of Slovokians and Mauritanians think their national governments as corrupt.

In 2015, even Americans' "trust and confidence in the wisdom of the American people when it comes to making political decisions"— that is to say, their trust in themselves—had fallen to just 34 percent, a thirty-point decline in less than 18 years. If "We the People" don't trust ourselves, our government, or our established political leaders to make decisions, who will we trust? The answer—at first for a plurality of Republican voters whose core adherents were authoritarians, and soon enough as his campaign gained momentum for a majority of all Republican voters—was Donald Trump. Said differently, their answer is a candidate whose message warned of American weakness and promised American renewal, and whose manner evinced strength as it disdained dissent.

---

124. Pew Research Center, "Beyond Distrust: How Americans View Their Government," November 23, 2015, http://www.people-press.org/files/2015/11/11-23-2015-Governance-release.pdf.

America's Choice: Is America's Authoritarian Spring a Harbinger of America's Fall?

In May of 2016 a man deep in thought focused on the equations jotted on a paper before him, ignoring his surroundings and oblivious to the rising concern of the woman sitting next to him on an airplane. What the woman thought she saw was a foreign-looking man writing in a language she didn't recognize or understand. She concluded he was a Muslim—and his scribblings a threat. She alerted a flight attendant.

The plane taxied back to the gate. The woman vacated her seat. And the man was asked to leave the plane. As he disembarked, he was met by a security agent who began to question him.

The man, a distinguished professor of economics at the University of Pennsylvania and a native of Italy, identified himself, showed the agent his mathematical musings, and was allowed to return to his seat. Describing the incident on social media, he wrote, "Trump's America is already here."[125] Win or lose in November, Donald Trump's campaign has left an indelible mark on America and American politics.

The authoritarian, ascriptive message of Donald Trump is not an anomaly in American history. However, its nationwide success in 2016 is a new, concerning development for Madisonian democracy, the protection of minority rights from majority tyranny, and the rule of law that protects individual rights. Trump's core support is firmly rooted in an American version of authoritarianism that, once awakened and stoked, is a force with which to be reckoned. Weakened and delegitimized, the institutions and leaders tasked with guarding against what Madison called "the infection of violent passions"[126] were either cowed by Trump's bluster or derelict in performing their civic duty. While Pat Buchanan, his demagogic predecessor, lost both of his campaigns for the Republican presidential nomination, Trump triumphed. Now, much of the Republican establishment has fallen in line behind Trump, appeasing him, putting political expediency before America's

---

125. Julie Shaw, "Passenger thinks Penn prof from Italy is terrorist, flight is delayed," *Philly.com*, May 9, 2016, http://www.philly.com/philly/news/20160508_Passenger_thinks_Penn_prof_doing_math_is__quot_terrorist__quot__flight_delayed.html.

126. James Madison, *The Federalist Papers* 63; The Avalon Project, Yale Law School, http://avalon.law.yale.edu/18th_century/fed63.asp.

tradition of republicanism and democratic liberalism, and placing on the table for this November the simple question: What type of society will America choose to become?

David Brooks has written that America's choice is now between an open or closed society.[127] Putting a finer point on his argument one month later, Brooks added: "We live in a big, diverse society. There are essentially two ways to maintain order and get things done in such a society—politics or some form of dictatorship. Either through compromise or brute force, our founding fathers chose politics."[128] Jonathan Freedland looked beyond the horizon to caution that the anger Trump is channeling in its most extreme form "threatens to shade into something darker: a revolt against the norms, the agreed boundaries that make democracy possible."[129]

But Rogers Smith, whose words served as the opening epigraph for this essay, reminds us of the other strong traditions that have animated America's political history:

A tradition…is comprised by (1) a worldview or ideology that defines basic political and economic institutions, the persons eligible to participate in them, and the roles or rights to which they are entitled and (2) institutions and practices embodying and reproducing those precepts. Hence traditions are not *merely* sets of ideas. The liberal tradition involves limited government, the rule of law protecting individual rights, and a market economy, all officially open to all minimally rational adults. The republican tradition is grounded on popular sovereignty exercised via institutions of mass self-governance. It includes an ethos of civic virtues and economic regulation for the public good.[130]

Democracy, of both liberal and republican sorts, is about compromise. Authoritarianism is us-versus-them. Authoritarian leaders do not compromise; they rule.

---

127. David Brooks, "Time for a Republican Conspiracy!," *New York Times*, January 19, 2016, http://www.nytimes.com/2016/01/19/opinion/time-for-a-republican-conspiracy.html.

128. David Brooks, "The Governing Cancer of Our Time," *New York Times*, February 26, 2016, http://www.nytimes.com/2016/02/26/opinion/the-governing-cancer-of-our-time.html.

129. Jonathan Freedland, "Welcome to the Age of Trump," *The Guardian*, May 19, 2016, http://www.theguardian.com/us-news/2016/may/19/welcome-to-the-age-of-trump.

130. Smith, "Beyond Tocqueville, Myrdal, and Hartz," 563, esp. footnote 4.

America's authoritarian spring is now past. But the question remains: Is it a harbinger of America's fall? Which path will Americans choose?

Appendix

Table 1:
Trump support among likely Republican primary voters by issue / characteristic

		Without Interaction Term	With Interaction Term
Authoritarianism		0.273 **	0.347 *
	Std. Err.	0.084	0.160
Terror Threat		0.150 **	0.212
	Std. Err.	0.053	0.124
Gender		-0.126	-0.126
	Std. Err..	0.200	0.200
Education		-0.415	-0.423
	Std. Err.	0.381	0.381
Age		-0.013	-0.009
	Std. Err..	0.433	0.433
Evangelicalism		0.025	0.035
	Std. Err.	0.214	0.215
Ideology		0.053	0.052
	Std. Err..	0.214	0.061
Church Attendance		-0.387	-0.385
	Std. Err.	0.220	0.220
Race		0.253	0.253
	Std. Err.	0.257	0.257
Income		-0.066	-0.058
	Std. Err.	0.437	0.437
Authoritarian*Terror			-0.604
	Std. Err.		1.099
Intercept		-1.917	-2.161
	Std. Err.	0.619	0.765
R-Squared		0.667	0.665
Adj. Count R-Squared		0.037	0.032
N		540	540

Source: University of Massachusetts Amherst, Political Science Department
December 10, 2015 National Survey
Note: Estimates Produced Using Logit Analysis
*p<.05, **p<.01, and ***p<.001

Table 2:
Authoritarianism and support for other Republican candidates among likely
Republican primary voters

		Cruz	Carson	Rubio	Bush
Authoritarianism		0.357	-0.028	0.091	-0.060
	Std. Err.	0.226	0.256	0.206	0.206
Terror Threat		0.367**	0.064	-0.074	-0.075
	Std. Err.	0.171	0.199	0.165	0.164
Gender		-0.276	-0.089	-0.480	0.443
	Std. Err.	0.291	0.320	0.319	0.307
Education		-0.075	-0.731	0.543	0.040
	Std. Err.	0.554	0.625	0.594	0.581
Age		-1.616**	1.956***	0.183	-1.575**
	Std. Err.	0.636	0.702	0.677	0.672
Evangelicalism		0.447	-0.326	-0.024	-0.506
	Std. Err.	0.308	0.338	0.341	0.361
Ideology		0.239**	0.07	0.031	-0.275***
	Std. Err.	0.102	0.094	0.096	0.093
Church Attendance		-0.062	0.947***	-0.528	-0.054
	Std. Err.	0.303	0.324	0.355	0.345
Race		-0.087	0.234	-0.392	0.644
	Std. Err.	0.370	0.407	0.342	0.343
Income		-0.251	0.753	0.588	0.682
	Std. Err.	0.616	0.725	0.659	0.664
Authoritarian*Terror		-4.008**	1.486	-0.049	0.193
	Std. Err.	1.637	1.714	1.624	1.542
Intercept		-3.175	-4.278	1.800	0.278
	Std. Err.	1.100	1.218	1.048	1.000
R-Squared		0.878	0.664	0.894	0.891
N		540	540	540	540

Source: University of Massachusetts Amherst, Political Science Department
December 10, 2015 National Survey
Note: Estimates Produced Using Logit Analysis
*p<.05, **p<.01, and ***p<.001

Selected Bibliography

Adorno, Theodor, Else Frenkel-Brunswick, Daniel J. Levinson, and Nevitt R. Sanford. *The Authoritarian Personality.* New York: Harper and Row, 1950.

Alexander, Michelle. *The New Jim Crow: Mass Incarceration in the Age of Colorblindness.* New York: The New Press, 2010.

Allport, Gordon W. "Attitudes." In Carl Murchison, ed. *The Handbook of Social Psychology.* Worcester, Mass.: Clark University Press, 1935.

Altemeyer, Robert. *The Authoritarians.* http://home.cc.umanitoba. ca/~altemey/

_____. *The Authoritarian Specter.* Cambridge: Harvard University Press, 1996.

_____. *Enemies of Freedom: Understanding Right-Wing Authoritarianism.* San Francisco: Jossey-Bass, 1988.

_____. *Right-Wing Authoritarianism.* Winnipeg: University of Manitoba Press, 1981.

Breyer, Stephen. *Making Our Democracy Work: A Judge's View.* New York: Alfred A. Knopf, 2010.

Buchanan, Patrick J. *State of Emergency: The Third World Invasion and Conquest of America.* New York: St. Martin's Press, 2006.

Carmines, Edward G. and James A. Stimson. *Issues Evolution: Race and the Transformation of American Politics.* Princeton, N.J.: Princeton University Press, 1989.

_____. "The Structure and Sequence of Issue Evolution." *American Political Science Review* 80 (1986): 901-920.

Christie, Richard. "Authoritarianism Re-Examined." In Richard Christie and Marie Jahoda, eds. *Studies in the Scope and Method of "The Authoritarian Personality": Continuities in Social Research.* Glencoe, Ill.: Free Press, 1954.

Cohen, Marty, David Karol, Hans Noel, and John Zaller. *The Party Decides: Presidential Nominations Before and After Reform.* Chicago: University of Chicago Press, 2008.

Dalton, Russell and Hans-Deiter Klingemann, eds. *Oxford Handbook of Political Behavior.* Oxford: Oxford University Press, 2007.

Davis, Darren and Brian Silver. "Exploring Black Political Intolerance." *Political Behavior* 17 (1) (1995),1-22.

Dawson, Michael. *Behind the Mule: Race and Class in African-American Politics.* Princeton: Princeton University Press, 1994.

Doty, Richardson, Bill Peterson, and David Winter. "Threat and Authoritarianism in the United States, 1978-1987." *Journal of Personality and Social Psychology* 61 (4) (1991), 629-640.

Duckitt, John. "Authoritarianism and Group Identification: A New View of an Old Construct." *Political Psychology* 10, no. 1 (1989): 63-84.

_____. *The Social Psychology of Prejudice.* New York: Praeger Press, 1992.

Feldman, Stanley. "Enforcing Social Conformity: A Theory of Authoritarianism." *Political Psychology* 24 (1) (2003), 41-74.

_____. "Values, Ideology, and the Structure of Political Attitudes." In David O. Sears, Leonie Huddy, and Robert Jervis, eds. *Oxford Handbook of Political Psychology.* New York: Oxford University Press, 2003.

Feldman, Stanley and Karen Stenner. "Perceived Threat and Authoritarianism." *Political Psychology* 18 (1997), 741-770.

Fillenbaum, Samuel and Arnold Jackman. "Dogmatism and Anxiety in Relation to Problem Solving: An Extension of Rokeach's Results." *The Journal of Abnormal and Social Psychology* 63 (1) (1961), 212-214.

Fischer, David H., *Albion's Seed: Four British Folkways in America.* New York: Oxford University Press, 1989.

Fromm, Erich. *Escape From Freedom.* New York: Henry Holt and Company, LLC., 1941.

_____. *Man for Himself: An Inquiry Into the Psychology of Ethics.* Oxford: Routledge, 1947.

Gabennesch, Howard. "Authoritarianism as World View." *American Journal of Sociology* 77 (5) (1972), 857-875.

Gibson, James. "A Sober Second Thought: An Experiment in Persuading Russians to Tolerate." *American Journal of Political Science* 42 (3) (1998), 819-850.

Greenberg, Jeff, Tom Pyszczynski, Sheldon Solomon, Abram Rosenblatt, Mitchell Veeder, Shari Kirkland, and Deborah Lyon. "Evidence for Terror Management Theory II: The Effects of Mortality Salience on Reactions to Those Who Threaten or Bolster the Cultural Worldview." *Journal of Personality and Social Psychology* 58 (2) (1990), 303-318.

Hamilton, Alexander, James Madison, John Jay, and Lawrence Goldman. *The Federalist Papers.* Oxford: Oxford University Press, 2008.

Hetherington, Marc and Elizabeth Suhay. "Authoritarianism, Threat, and Americans' Support for the War on Terror." *American Journal of Political Science* 55 (3) (2011): 546-560.

Hetherington, Marc and Jonathan Weiler. *Authoritarianism and Polarization in American Politics.* Cambridge: Cambridge University Press, 2009.

Hofstadter, Richard. "The Paranoid Style in American Politics." *Harper's Magazine* 229 (1374) (1964), 77-86.

Hyman, Herbert and Paul B. Sheatsley. "The Authoritarian Personality—A Methodological Critique." In Richard Christie and Marie Jahoda, eds. *Studies in the Scope and Method of "The Authoritarian Personality": Continuities in Social Research.* Glencoe, Ill.: Free Press, 1954.

Jost, John T., Jack Glaser, Arie W. Kruglanski, and Frank J. Sulloway. "Political Conservatism as Motivated Social Cognition," *Psychological Bulletin* 129 (2003), 339-375.

Kinder, Donald R. and Cindy D. Kam. *Us Against Them: Ethnocentric Foundations of American Opinion.* Chicago: University of Chicago Press, 2009.

Lavine, Howard, Milton Lodge, James Polichak, and Charles Taber. "Explicating the Black Box Through Experimentation: Studies of Authoritarianism and Threat." *Political Analysis* 10 (4) (2002), 343-361.

Lavine, Howard, Milton Lodge, and Kate Freitas. "Threat, Authoritarianism, and Selective Exposure to Information." *Political Psychology* 26 (2005), 219-244.

Lipset, Seymour M. "Democracy and Working-Class Authoritarianism." *American Sociological Review* 24 (4) (1959), 482-501.

_____. *Political Man: The Social Bases of Politics*. Garden City, N.Y.: Doubleday, 1960.

MacWilliams, Matthew C. *American Authoritarianism in Black and White*. Dissertation: University of Massachusetts Amherst, 2016.

Marcus, George E., Elizabeth Thciss-Morse, John L. Sullivan, Sandra L. Wood. *With Malice Toward Some: How People Make Civil Liberties Judgments*. Cambridge. Cambridge University Press, 1995.

McFarland, Sam G. and Vladimir S. Ageyev. "Economic Threat and Authoritarianism in the United States and Russia." Paper presented at the Annual Meeting of the International Society for Political Psychology. Washington, D.C., 1995.

Meloen, Jos D. "The F-scale as a Predictor of Fascism: An Overview of 40 Years of Authoritarianism Research." In William F. Stone, Gerda Lederer, and Richard Christie, eds. *Strength and Weakness: The Authoritarian Personality Today*. New York: Springer, 1993.

Meloen, Jos D., Gert Van der Linden, and Hans De Witte. "A Test of the Approaches of Adorno et al., Lederer and Altemeyer of Authoritarianism in Belgian Flanders: A Research Note." *Political Psychology* 17 (4) (1996), 643-656.

Myers, David G. *Social Psychology* (10th edition). Boston: McGraw-Hill, 2010.

Pérez, Efrén O. and Marc J. Hetherington. "Authoritarianism in Black and White: Testing the Cross-Racial Validity of the Child Rearing Scale." *Political Analysis* 22 (3) (2014), 398-412.

Ray, John J. "The Development and Validation of a Balanced Dogmatism Scale." *Australian Journal of Psychology* 22 (3) (1970), 253-260.

_____. "Half of All Authoritarians Are Left Wing: A Reply to Eysenck and Stone." *Political Psychology* 4 (1) (1983), 139-143.

_____. "A New Balanced F Scale and Its Relation to Social Class." *Australian Psychologist* 7 (3) (1972), 155-166.

Rickert, Edward J. "Authoritarianism and Economic Threat: Implications for Political Behavior." *Political Psychology* 19 (4) (1998), 707-720.

Rokeach, Milton. *The Open and Closed Mind.* Oxford: Basic Books, 1960.

Sales, Stephen M. "Threat as a Factor in Authoritarianism: An Analysis of Archival Data." *Journal of Personality and Social Psychology* 28 (1) (1973), 44-57.

Sales, Stephen M. and Kenneth E. Friend. "Success and Failure as Determinants of Level of Authoritarianism." *Behavioral Science* 18 (3) (1973), 163-172.

Sanford, Nevitt. *Self and Society: Social Change and Individual Development.* New York: Atherton Press, 1966.

Schwartz, Tony. *The Responsive Chord.* Garden City, N.Y.: Anchor Press/Doubleday, 1973.

Shils, Edward A. "Authoritarianism: Right and Left." In Richard Christie and Marie Jahoda, eds. *Studies in the Scope and Method of "The Authoritarian Personality": Continuities in Social Research.* Glencoe, Ill.: Free Press, 1954.

Smith, Charles U. and James W. Prothro. "Ethnic Differences in Authoritarian Personality." *Social Forces* 35 (4) (1957), 334-338.

Smith, Rogers M. "Beyond Tocqueville, Myrdal, and Hartz: The Multiple Traditions in America." *American Political Science Review* 87 (3) (1993), 549-566.

Stenner, Karen. *The Authoritarian Dynamic.* Cambridge: Cambridge University Press, 2005.

Sullivan, John L., James Piereson, and George E. Marcus. *Political Tolerance and American Politics: The Empirical Literature.* Chicago: University of Chicago Press, 1993.

Tate, Katherine. *From Protest to Politics: The New Black Voters in American Elections.* Cambridge, Mass.: Harvard University Press, 1994.

Wilson, Glenn D. The Psychology of Conservatism. New York: Academic Press, 1973.

Wilson, Glenn D. and John R. Patterson. "A New Measure of Conservatism." *British Journal of Social and Clinical* Psychology 7 (4) (1968), 264–269.

Wolfe, Alan. "'The Authoritarian Personality' Revisited." *Chronicle of Higher Education* 52 (7) (October 7, 2005), B12.

Wronski, Julie. "Authoritarianism & Social Identity Sorting: Exploring the Sources of American Mass Partisanship." Prepared for the National Capital American Political Science Association Meeting, Washington, DC, January 5, 2015.

CPSIA information can be obtained at www.ICGtesting.com
Printed in the USA
BVIW12n2302161016
464940BV00001B/1